Buds
&
Blossoms

Delicious and beautiful edible flower recipes

Buds & Blossoms

LIZ KNIGHT

Hardie Grant
BOOKS

Introduction

I was born in the late 1970s and like many children of that era, I grew up in a pebble-dashed house alongside the requisite crazy-paved patio. Rising from the broken concrete slabs were a number of dangerously nailed together posts, which if you were short sighted, you might've called a pergola. During the winter, the posts were only kept from tumbling to the ground by a gnarly climbing rose that somehow held the wooden structure together. Devoid of leaves or flowers, covered in inch-long hooked thorns, it was hardly the most welcoming of sights. But, come early summer, the tangle of thorns transformed into a fragrant archway that dripped in plate-sized floribunda roses, the kind that only suited pink pebble-dashed semis in the early 1980s. The roses may have been gaudy, but they smelt like something far more ethereal, delicious even – I desperately wanted to eat the apricot pink flowers, but had no idea that I could. Instead, I pushed the petals into bottles to make perfume, and pounded the flowers into a pulp which was then stirred into handfuls of the thick clay soil of our garden, making the most fragrant of mud pies. I may have been the archetypal bored 1980s 7-year-old, sat in an archetypal suburban garden, but my play could have been mirroring a child from a far less synthetic era – deep in the Indus valley where rose petals were packed into clay pots to make fragrant rose water – the remains of which helped archaeologists build a picture of the sophistication of one of the oldest known civilizations on the planet.

Years later, when I discovered that roses were indeed food (and every bit as delicious as I hoped my mud pies would taste). I started growing my own roses to cook with; and as anyone who gardens will know, plants are addictive, so it wasn't long before my roses were interplanted with primroses, hostas and a little magnolia sapling. One by one I discovered that, like the roses around my parents' pergola, these plants and many of the others I squeezed into every inch of my garden were also edible. Not just edible, but delicious.

Over the years I've eaten my way around not just my garden, but the gardens of friends and neighbours, eating the flowers, leaves, seeds, and even roots of plants most people consider to be ornamental rather than edible. Choosing just 20 plants to write about was like having to pick a favourite child, when you love them all. The plants featured in this book have been chosen because they are delicious and easy to grow. Even if you only have a balcony with a pot, most of them can be grown in limited spaces (even water lilies thrive in small ponds), turning the smallest spaces into a beautiful, edible garden.

If gardening is less appealing than cooking, fear not, many of the plants featured are available to buy on the high street – jars of dried rose petals, lavender, sumac and saffron line even the least exciting supermarket shelves. Even the more unusual ingredients are just a click away – Japanese food speciality retailers sell magnolia leaves for example, Indian supermarkets will have water lily seeds and even fresh jasmine flowers and an increasing number of edible flower growers supply everything from roses to peonies to lilac blooms.

Who knows, hopefully you'll be inspired to plant and start growing your own edible ornamental patch – whether you have a few pots on a balcony or a back garden with a rickety pergola.

A WORD OF CAUTION (HOW TO EAT YOUR GARDEN)

Before you head outside and munch on everything in sight, make sure that you do your research on whether a plant (and the specific variety) you have is edible – some plants are incredibly toxic, even deadly. Make sure that any plants you buy to eat have not been treated with chemicals – if you can't find out for sure, then plant your purchase and let them grow in your garden for at least a season (longer if you are harvesting from the roots) before harvesting anything from them.

Just as some people are intolerant or allergic to farmed foods, so some people are allergic to different edible garden plants. When you first eat new plants, introduce small amounts of them to your diets to make sure that you don't have any side effects. If you have a medical condition or are pregnant, research whether the plants you are wanting to eat are safe with your condition or medication.

Preserving Your Garden

There aren't many better times to eat your flowers than when they are freshly blooming all around you, but it's also really rather lovely to be able to eat memories of those warm summer days when you're in the depths of winter. To that end, here are some of the ways you can preserve your buds and blossoms.

CANDYING

Candying or sugaring flowers is a lovely way to preserve flowers – you can also candy edible leaves.

SYRUP

Capturing the essence of flowers in a syrup requires a light touch where you must avoid scalding the flowers. Infuse your blooms in a warm syrup for a few hours. Strain the infused syrup before reheating and pouring into sterilised bottles. White cane sugar makes the best base for floral syrups – unrefined sugars tend to have a slight molasses taste and detract from the flavour of the flowers. A very lightly flavoured honey is the best alternative if you want to avoid processed sugars but it will have a definite honey flavour. Keep your syrups out of direct sunlight to preserve their colour and flavour for as long as possible (floral syrups can keep for up to a year).

LIQUEURS

Flowers are beautiful captured in sweet liqueurs; be swift when infusing flowers as alcohol will not only pull out the delicate floral perfume and flavour of your flowers, but after a short time will start to extract the more medicinal, tannic properties – often just an hour or two of infusion time will give you a bright, fragrant flavour. Strain the flowers out through a coffee filter as soon as your drink tastes floral. A note on the type of spirit to infuse your flowers into: whilst neutral spirits like vodka, grappa and eau de vie are most commonly used, adding flowers to a stronger-tasting base like brandy, rum or tequila can give the drink a rounded, honeyed flavour.

VINEGARS

Apple cider vinegar, white wine vinegar and rice wine vinegar make perfect bases to infuse floral flavours in. Most floral vinegars will benefit from a slight sweetness. However, as with syrups, to ensure your flowers are the hero flavour, use white sugar or a very mild honey as unrefined sugars or dark honeys will give the vinegar a molasses flavour which detracts from the taste of the delicate flowers.

DRYING

Many edible flowers dry incredibly well, but be aware that drying will always slightly change their flavour, making them best used in conjunction with other ingredients such as herbs or spices. To dry your flowers, gather them on a dry day (if you are in a dusty, polluted area, rinse the flowers in cold water before drying them in a salad spinner) – you want to start dehydrating with flowers which are as dry as possible.

Lay your single flowers out on a dehydrating tray or on a clean cloth on a baking rack if you don't have a dehydrator. Dry them on the lowest setting (around 40°C/100°F) until they are crumbly – be aware that flowers will often rehydrate in the humidity of the air, so as soon as they reach that crumble-dry texture, place them into an airtight container and store out of direct sunlight for up to 12 months (until the next year's harvest).

SALTING

Preserving flowers in salt is an easy way to make seasonings. There are two ways to preserve flowers in salt: firstly by dehydrating the flower (around 40°C/100°F for 10 hours) and stirring it through the salt – this keeps the colours of the flowers bright and clear, but the flavour of the flowers will remain in the flowers rather than transfer into the salt. The second method is to blend fresh flowers and salt with a splash of water – use a food processor and blend until the salt and flowers have become a coloured paste. Lay this salt out on a baking tray and place in a very low oven to dry out; the salt will have absorbed the flavour of the flowers providing a more complex flavour.

SUGAR

Preserving flowers in sugar is a more fail-safe way to preserve flowers in a sweet way than in syrups. Place the flowers between layers of white sugar and cover with a final coating of sugar. Cover and leave to sit overnight – the fresh oils in the flowers will start to infuse into the sugar making it slightly damp. The next day, blend the flowers and sugar to a fine powder in a food processor; spread onto a dish and dry completely before storing in airtight jars. Sugars will keep for up to a year and can be used in baking or dissolved into liquid and used as a syrup when needed.

FREEZING

Perhaps the simplest way to preserve flowers to use later in the year is to freeze them – this is especially worth doing for flowers that you are to use as an ingredient rather than to use as a garnish, given that when the flowers are removed from the freezer, they will invariably start to break up and wilt as they thaw. However, if you want to use them to make syrup, vinegar or even to flavour creams and cakes, you can simply tip the flowers into your liquid. Should you want to keep flecks of the flowers in your recipe – say suspended through a jelly dessert or ice cream – you can crumble flowers whilst they are still frozen into tiny flecks far easier than if the flowers were fresh.

FERMENTING

You can add flowers to a wide range of ferments: from drinks such as kombucha, kefir and lightly alcoholic 'champagnes' and boozier wine, to adding handfuls to savoury ferments such as kimchi or sauerkraut. Using flowers in this way can lose the distinct flavour of the flower but it captures and even boosts their nutritional benefits. These ferments are by their nature unpasteurised and will keep fermenting, so once you have reached your desired flavours store them in the refrigerator and eat within a few weeks (remembering to release the gases that build up to avoid a messy accident).

JAMS AND JELLIES

Flowers can be transformed into beautiful condiments, either infused as a flavour (such as in the apple and lavender jelly) or suspended through a preserve as a jam. Apple pectin is an ideal base ingredient for making floral jellies, but lots of other fruits also pair deliciously with flowers, especially when blended with ingredients that are in season at the same time. Try mixing magnolia or lilac with forced rhubarb, primrose with lemon, rose petals with raspberries or wisteria with strawberries.

A NOTE ON SUCCESSFUL STORING

Whatever preservation technique you use, to successfully store flowers it is important to have squeaky clean equipment and containers. They must be airtight to stop moisture from building up.

Use really hot water, soap and a good brush to remove any residue on the bottles or jars, especially if they are used. Then run your clean equipment through the dishwasher on its hottest setting, just before you fill the bottles or jars to make sure they are completely clean.

Select the right lids for the job. Alcohol, vinegar and even salt can corrode metal lids, so make sure you seal your jars with the right lids for your ingredients.

FLAVOUR PROFILE

Camellia blossoms are astringent, with flavours of cardamom, lemon zest and mild chicory. The leaves taste like green tea when fresh, and a less tannic black tea when fermented and dried.

Camellia

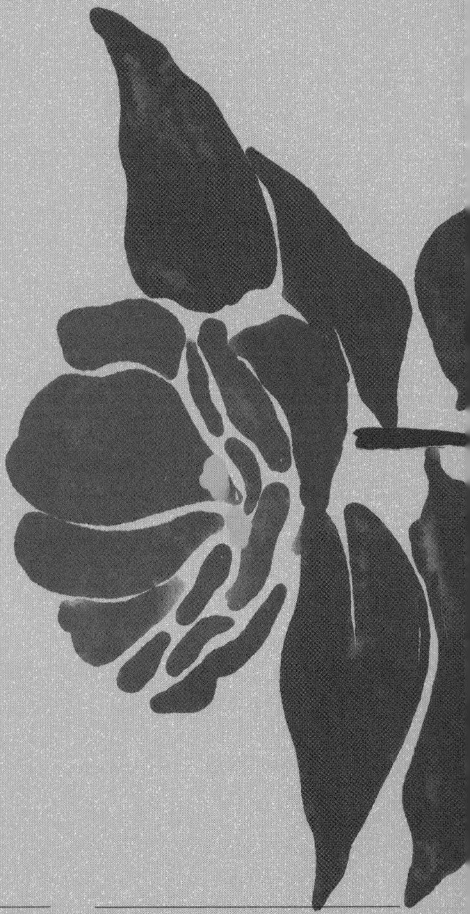

COMMONLY USED EDIBLE SPECIES

Camellia sinensis (tea plant), *Camellia japonica* (Japanese camellia), *Camellia sasanqua* (sasanqua camellia), *Camellia reticulata* (Yunnan camellia), *Camellia oleifera* (oil-seed camellia).

WHERE THEY GROW

Camellias thrive in dappled shade and acidic soils (if your soil is alkaline they are best grown in pots of ericaceous compost). Try to protect camellias from cold winds or harsh sun – *Camellia sinensis* requires even more protection and is best moved inside in the winter.

WHEN TO GATHER

Leaves – all year (select new growth to harvest)

Flowers – autumn (fall) through to mid-spring (some species flower in the summer)

If you're reading this with a cup of tea by your side, you have the camellia plant to thank for your brew, and potentially Chinese Emperor Shennong (considered the father of Chinese herbal medicine). Legend has it that in 2737 BC, the Emperor sat waiting for water to boil when a camellia leaf fell into the vessel. Being a herbally curious type of person he decided to partake of the drink. In that moment he changed drinking history with the first cup of camellia tea. Of course, if he'd been a tea master, he would've known that it was sacrilege to make tea with boiling water, but it was the first ever cup, so we should show the poor man some leniency.

PARTS USED

① Flowering buds
② Petals
③ Leaves (twigs and bark used in traditional herbal medicinal tea)

At the start of tea's journey to become what it is today, fresh or dried camellia leaves were simply added to water and drunk. However, the tea we know today came about as a result of another accident, this time trying to produce and preserve enough of the leaves to slake China's growing thirst for the drink. By 1600, demand for tea in China was so immense that factories heating, crushing and fermenting the leaves produced vast amounts of teas, which were all still more like green tea. One of these factories was in the process of making tea when a troop of soldiers inconveniently disrupted the process and the delicate tea leaves were left for too long, turning black with fermentation. And so black tea was born, the most common hot drink in the world.

It was *Camellia sinensis* that fell into that fateful cup of Emperor Shennong, which led it to being crowned the true tea, but it could have been so different. Had the leaf from another type of camellia dropped into his drink you might have been sipping on that right now – and the world map of tea production would've looked very different. *Camellia sinensis* is a tender and rather particular type, requiring just the right conditions to thrive, which is why you don't find tea gardens in many climates. Other camellias, as you might know from the shrub in your garden, are far hardier affairs, not only surviving but flowering through the bleakest winter moments. Perhaps if a different camellia fell into the pot, you'd now find tea plantations next to potato and wheat fields.

Hardy camellia plants are mainly grown for their robust survival skills, providing gardeners with evergreen foliage and winter flowers to look at; their potential for food and drink forgotten but still there. Not only are the leaves of all camellias edible, their crunchy winter flowers are full of bite, bitterness and hints of cardamom and citrus. Camellia flowers are delicious added to winter salads, turning them into the most spirit-lifting floral affairs at a time when blooms are in short supply. They also make a fantastic ingredient for kimchi-style ferments and, of course, floral teas.

Once the flowers drop, camellias start to produce seeds full of edible oils. Tea-seed oil is widely used in Southeast Asia for good reason, not only does it have a high smoking point, making it the perfect oil for frying food, but it also lowers cholesterol, and has more antioxidants than most other oils, along with high levels of vitamin E, heart-beneficial monounsaturated acids, and the holy trinity of omega 3, 6 and 9 fats. Obviously, to make a bottle of oil, you'll need a lot more camellia seeds to press than you most likely have on your garden shrub, so it's probably worth buying a bottle of the oil ready to add to your food.

What you will have in abundance if you have a camellia shrub are the leaves, which like their tea-leaf sibling benefit from a bit of rolling, steaming and fermenting to bring out the best in them as an ingredient. They can be fried in slivers to top rice, dried and ground into a chai-inspired spice blend, or even used to smoke food. And of course, you could make them into one last thing – a good old-fashioned cup of tea.

SERVES 4

Camellia Leaf Broth with Fried Sushi Rice Balls

Inspired by Japanese *ochazuke*, a comforting bowl of green tea over rice, camellia leaves make a beautiful broth and seasoning for toasted sushi balls. Using fermented and fresh camellia leaves gives a rounded flavour to the dish and the finely sliced and fried fresh leaves adds a delicious seasoning to the bowl of broth and toasted rice.

2 tbsp rolled camellia tea (see page 22) or 2 tsp green tea
10 fresh camellia leaves
250 g (9 oz/generous 1 cup) sushi rice
vegetable oil, for frying
pinch of salt
2 tsp nigella seeds
pinch of chilli (hot pepper) flakes
light soy sauce, to taste
2 spring onions (scallions), finely sliced
1 seared duck breast or 250 g (9 oz) smoked salmon, sliced, to serve (optional)

Place the dried camellia tea (or green tea) and fresh camellia leaves in a teapot or lidded bowl and pour over a cup of just-boiled water (enough to cover the leaves). Leave to infuse for 30 minutes.

Meanwhile, wash the sushi rice in a bowl until the water runs clear, then leave to soak for 30 minutes.

Drain the rice and place in a pan along with 350 ml (12 fl oz/scant 1½ cups) fresh water. Bring to the boil, then turn the heat down low, cover and cook for 10–12 minutes or until the water is absorbed. The rice should be tender and sticky enough to mould. With wet hands, roll the rice into golf-ball-sized spheres.

Fry the rice balls in a splash of oil until golden. Set aside.

Remove the whole, fresh camellia leaves from the tea and finely slice into grass-like slivers. Heat 1 tablespoon of oil in the frying pan and fry the leaves until crispy. Transfer to a bowl and mix with the salt, nigella seeds and chilli flakes.

Reheat the camellia tea. Place the sushi balls in a serving bowl and pour over the hot camellia tea, season with soy sauce and top with the fried camellia leaf seasoning and spring onions. Serve by itself or topped with slices of duck or salmon.

SERVES 4

Camellia-leaf Smoked Chicken

Smoking chicken with tea originated in the Sichuan region of Northern China, but it's now a technique used by fans of smoked foods across the world. Not only does smoking give food a unique flavour, it also helps keep meat moist and tender. You can use most teas to smoke with – the leaves of camellias like *japonica* give a more subtle, light flavour to chicken than traditional tea.

2 tbsp Sichuan peppercorns
2 tsp salt
5 tbsp dried fermented camellia leaves (or black tea)
4 chicken legs, skin on
2 tbsp brown sugar
2 tbsp rice
sesame oil, for brushing

Place the Sichuan peppercorns, salt and 2 tablespoons of the camellia tea leaves into a spice grinder and grind to a powder. Rub the powder over the chicken legs and refrigerate overnight.

The next day, place the chicken in a steamer and steam until the chicken is just cooked and the juices in the chicken run clear, around 15–20 minutes. Leave to cool.

To smoke the chicken you will need a pan with a tight-fitting lid (ideally cast iron) and a trivet or steamer. Line the bottom of the pan with a few layers of foil, place on top of the foil a blend of the remaining camellia tea leaves, brown sugar and rice. Place a metal rack above the mixture and place the chicken legs onto the rack. Cover the pan with the lid and place over a gentle heat until smoke starts coming out of the pan. Smoke the chicken for 10 minutes before turning off the heat. Leave covered for 20 minutes before removing the pan lid.

Remove the chicken from the trivet, brush with sesame oil and serve with rice and greens.

Pickled Camellia and Turnips

Radishes and turnips often pretend to be camellia flowers. In Japan you can buy camellia sushi, which isn't actually camellia but the dyed vegetables, which are formed into the shape of the flower and wrapped around sushi rice, often eaten as camellias burst into flower. There's a lot to be said for pickled turnips, but there's also a lot to write home about when it comes to pickled camellia flowers. Placing the interloper and the authentic camellia together in a pickle turns out to be a marriage made in pickle heaven. You can either eat this pickle as a palate cleanser, as part of a meal or wrapped around balls of sushi as a genuine camellia sushi.

MAKES 1 JAR OF PICKLES

2 medium turnips
1 tsp salt
120 ml (4 fl oz/½ cup) rice wine vinegar
1 tsp sugar
½ tsp black peppercorns, crushed
3 thin slices of fresh root ginger
petals from 6 camellia flowers

Peel the turnips, then thinly slice with a mandoline or side slicer on a box grater. Toss the slices in a bowl with the salt and leave for 30 minutes, or until liquid drains into the bottom of the bowl.

While the turnips are soaking, place the vinegar, sugar, pepper and ginger slices in a saucepan and heat until the sugar dissolves.

Add the camellia flowers to the turnips, making sure to coat them in the salty brine before draining away any liquid and packing the turnips and petals into a clean jar. Pour over the vinegar solution and seal with a non-reactive lid. Place in the refrigerator and keep for up to a week.

Camellia Blossom Salad with Cardamom Dressing

Camellia flowers have a gentle sour citrus flavour with a hint of cardamom. Their early spring flowers coincide with the peak season for bitter radicchio and chicory, and together with this cardamom-infused salad dressing they make a vibrant, fragrant salad in an otherwise hungry gap. It is lovely served with goat's cheese or grilled chicken.

SERVES 6

FOR THE DRESSING

1 lemon: zest of ½ and juice of whole
1 tsp honey
2 tbsp olive oil
¼ tsp ground cardamom
salt and black pepper, to taste

FOR THE SALAD

1 fennel bulb
½ radicchio
1 chicory
2 crisp sharp apples
100 g (3½ oz) spinach
petals from 2 camellia flowers

Place all the dressing ingredients in a jar and shake to combine. Leave the dressing to infuse for 30 minutes before using.

Finely slice the fennel, radicchio, chicory and apples. Place in a bowl with the spinach and toss in the dressing.

Transfer to a serving platter and scatter over the individual camellia petals to serve.

How to Make Tea with Camellia Leaves

Green, black and matcha tea are all made from the leaves of *Camellia sinensis*, but other camellia leaves can be processed in exactly the same way to make a tea that is slightly less tannic and astringent but more floral tasting; more suited to drinking without milk than a builders' brew. In just a few steps you can turn your prunings into a home-grown cuppa.

To make green tea leaves, harvest the top young leaves on the new spring growth. It's best to gather the leaves in the morning. Spread the freshly gathered leaves out on a cloth and let them wither for a few hours. Gently heat a wok and drop the leaves into the warm pan, turning the leaves constantly until they become hot to the touch (you need to move them continually or they may burn). As soon as the leaves are hot, pour them out of the pan onto a cool surface. Spread out the leaves to cool, then roll them between your hands to break open the cells. Place the rolled leaves on a baking sheet in a very low oven for a few hours (around 60°C/140°F/gas ¼) until they are crumbly and completely dry.

To make black tea leaves, you can harvest older leaves as well as younger ones. Let the leaves wither for 24 hours, then roll between your hands as with the green tea. Spread the rolled leaves out and leave somewhere warm. They will start to oxidise and turn brown. Dry in a low oven (50°C/120°F) or dehydrator for a few hours until the leaves have thoroughly dried out; store in an airtight jar. Tea stored properly will last indefinitely but it will taste best in the first year.

MAKES 20

Spiced Camellia Tea Biscuits

There's not much more comforting in life than tea and biscuits, especially if those biscuits are flavoured with just enough warming spices to give a hint of warm cosy evenings. Nordic winters are all about comfort, or *hygge*, and there won't be many homes in that part of the world that don't bake some spiced pepper biscuits to warm spirits at that time of year. Blitzing tea (store-bought or home-grown) to a fine powder with pepper and other warming spices makes a blend that smells of all things cosy, and makes biscuits worth pulling a blanket over your knees and cuddling a steaming mug of tea with. This recipe will make a small jar of spice that, as well as for baking, can be used to make chai with warm milk (just add a couple of cardamom pods) or rubbed onto pork belly before it has a slow, aromatic cook.

FOR THE CAMELLIA TEA SPICE BLEND

- 10 g (½ oz) fermented dried camellia tea leaves
- 4 cloves
- 5 g (¼ oz/2 tsp) ground cinnamon
- 2 g (⅔ tsp) ground cardamom
- 1 g (⅓ tsp) ground mace or nutmeg
- 1 g (⅓ tsp) ground coriander
- 1 g (½ tsp) black peppercorns

FOR THE BISCUITS

- 125 g (4½ oz) butter, at room temperature
- 50 g (1¾ oz/scant ¼ cup) granulated sugar
- 50 g (1¾ oz/generous ⅛ cup) golden syrup
- 1 egg
- 210 g (7½ oz/1½ cups) plain (all-purpose) flour
- 1 tsp baking powder
- 2 heaped tsp camellia tea spice blend (see above)

For the camellia tea spice blend, place the tea leaves and all the spices in a small spice grinder and grind to a powder. Store in a jar.

For the biscuits, cream the butter and sugar together until fluffy and light, then beat in the golden syrup and egg.

In a separate bowl, sift together the flour, baking powder and the spice blend and mix until thoroughly combined. Add the butter, sugar and egg mixture, stirring it into a soft dough. Place the dough on a piece of greaseproof paper and form into a log, then flatten slightly into a lozenge shape, wrap tightly and refrigerate overnight.

Preheat the oven to 180°C (350°F/gas 4).

Slice 5 mm (¼ in) discs from the dough lozenge. Place on a lined baking sheet and bake for 7 minutes, or until a pale golden colour. The biscuits will firm up when they are cooling (if they aren't eaten before they cool down).

Serve with (camellia) tea.

FLAVOUR PROFILE

FLOWERS Usually ginger or cardamom, some have hints of lemon and nutmeg.

LEAVES Lemongrass

TWIGS Cardamom

Magnolia

COMMONLY USED EDIBLE SPECIES

Magnolia coco (coconut magnolia), *Magnolia grandiflora* (southern magnolia), *Magnolia denudata* (Yulan magnolia), *Magnolia kobus* (kobushi magnolia), *Magnolia mexicana* (Mexican magnolia), *Magnolia pterocarpa* (winged magnolia), *Magnolia* x *soulangeana* (saucer magnolia).

WHERE THEY GROW

Full sun or partial shade in neutral or slightly acidic soil.

WHEN TO GATHER

Deciduous species flower in early to mid-spring; evergreens bloom from summer until autumn (fall). Leaves can be collected from spring (when green and tender) until they fall in the autumn (dried brown).

Springtime in towns and cities arrives in style; the muted tones of winter coats replaced with vibrant dresses and short sleeves. And, just as the best dressed in town can't wait for an excuse to don elegant clothes, the bare branches of magnolia trees are suddenly adorned with thousands of petals. For a couple of weeks magnolia trees transform the dullest streets into nature's version of a spring catwalk show. If trees had designers, magnolia trees would have been created by the most flamboyant, attention-grabbing of them all.

PARTS USED

① Flowering buds
② Petals
③ Leaves (twigs and bark used in traditional herbal medicinal tea)

Since as early as the 16th century, European plant hunters fell in love with the floral muses, collecting them from both Asia and the Americas. The early-flowering trees with porcelain petals and pineapple-shaped carpel centres must have seemed otherworldly to Europeans, but magnolias were in fact making a return visit to the continent. Millions of years previously, before the cold winds of the Eocene Ice Age blew over Europe, magnolias grew as a wild species across the continent. The magnolias that plant hunters brought from the Americas may have arrived by boat, but the first magnolia trees spread from their North American origins by land migration. They are such an incredibly ancient species that they grew across the supercontinent of Pangea before it broke apart and the new land masses drifted across the globe.

Magnolias haven't altered much in the millions of years they've been on the ever-changing earth – 112-million-year-old fossils found in Kansas, North America, show ancestors of the trees with the same characteristics we'd recognise in the trees in our gardens. Their large petals and pineapple-like carpels are thanks to their incredible age, blooming during an era when flying pollinators like bees were but a twinkle in Mother Nature's eye. Magnolias relied on far older, weightier pollinators – beetles, who would climb into the fragrant flowers transferring pollen from one flower to another, allowing the tips of branches to grow fruits full of bright red seeds that would produce the next generation of tree (unless an inconsiderate ice age froze them into extinction).

And just like the last ice age wiped out Europe's magnolia trees, so a cold night can see a tree that was covered in flamboyant flowers in the evening become bare the next morning, the ground below carpeted in petals, bruised from their chilly fall. The demise of the beautiful floral decorations comes with some comfort at least, because the fallen petals can be dried and ground into a warming spice with hints of nutmeg and ginger (even petals turning brown from the chill).

If you are able to gather your perfect flowers before a frost hits, you'll discover that these fleshy petals have not only the most satisfying crunchy texture, but are also filled with incredible flavour. According to the species of magnolia flower you bite into, you'll find everything from ginger to cardamom, chicory, and even hints of lemongrass. Summer-flowering *grandiflora* flowers smell like the sweetest of lemon possets and taste intensely like bitter lemon oil – used sparingly, the flowers make a delicious flavouring for puddings and liqueurs.

In Central America, Aztecs paired *Magnolia mexicana* flowers with chilli, vanilla and nutmeg to flavour their rich chocolate drinks over 2,500 years ago. Meanwhile, in China, the flower buds, known as *yu-lan-hua-pian*, were given more savoury treatment, pickled with vinegar and ginger, and eaten with rice. In the Sichuan province, where magnolias spread high up into the mountains, their flowers like drifts of pink-tinged snow covering the hillsides in early spring, they are gathered and deep-fried in sweet batter. These battered flowers make for a beautiful spring dessert, especially dunked into Aztec-inspired melted chocolate drinks – like a floral churro.

If you're not a fan of fried food, you can use the flowers as a receptacle for all kinds of other delicious flavours. Try stuffing the flowers with vanilla-sweetened soft cheeses, or sprinkle over a crumbled ginger biscuit, and serve alongside some poached rhubarb to make an early spring pudding that even Montezuma would be tempted to choose over his chocolate drink.

It is not only the flowers of the magnolia tree that can be used to make food taste more delicious, the leaves are also edible. The fragrant leaves of *Magnolia mexicana* were also added to chocolate as a flavouring just as the flowers were. Known as *hoba* in Japan, the leaves are stuffed with ingredients and heated over fire in order to infuse their fragrance into the food.

And magnolia's usefulness doesn't end there – even the twigs and bark of the tree have a far more worthwhile function than just being a frame for flowers. In both Chinese and Mexican traditional herbal medicines, these less-showy parts of the magnolia have been used for a wide range of treatments, including the alleviation of stress – probably best prescribed alongside a big slab of magnolia-flower-infused chocolate.

SERVES 4

Magnolia Stuffed with Spiced Mushrooms

Magnolia flower flavours come alive with just a few moments of cooking and turn from crunchy petals to translucent wraps for dumpling-style fillings. Don't panic if the flowers you are stuffing are slightly bruised, since any imperfections disappear as the flowers cook. Pair the parcels with a beautiful dipping sauce made with the raw petals.

2 tbsp sunflower oil, plus extra for shallow-frying
8 spring onions (scallions), finely chopped
3 garlic cloves, finely chopped
thumb-sized piece of fresh root ginger, grated
350 g (12 oz) chestnut (cremini) mushrooms, pulsed in a blender into small pieces
1 tsp Chinese five spice
¼ tsp chilli (hot pepper) flakes
¼ tsp black pepper
200 g (7 oz) spinach, shredded
3 tbsp light soy sauce
2 tbsp rice vinegar
2 tbsp mirin (or white wine vinegar with 1 tsp sugar)
8 open magnolia flower heads, each with a piece of stalk attached

FOR THE DIPPING SAUCE

60 ml (2 fl oz/¼ cup) light soy sauce
60 ml (2 fl oz/¼ cup) rice wine vinegar
2½ tsp sugar
½ shallot, finely chopped
2 tsp grated fresh root ginger
½ tsp sesame oil
pinch of chilli (hot pepper) flakes
1 magnolia flower head

Heat the sunflower oil in a saucepan over a low heat, add half of the spring onions along with the garlic and ginger, and sweat until the onions are soft. Add the mushrooms, five spice, chilli flakes and pepper along with the spinach, and cook until almost dry, stirring frequently to prevent burning. Once most of the liquid has evaporated, add the soy, vinegar and mirin, and reduce again until the mixture is glossy and not sitting in any liquid. Remove from the heat and allow to cool.

While the filling is cooling, rinse the magnolia flowers, and remove any badly damaged, wilted petals (petals that are slightly browning are still fine to use). Carefully lift the top 3 petals and spoon in enough of the filling so that you can fold the petals back to create a closed flower effect. Fill all of the flowers in this way, then set aside.

Make the dipping sauce by mixing together the soy sauce, vinegar and sugar with the shallot, ginger, sesame oil and chilli flakes. Finely slice the magnolia petals into grass-like slivers and stir into the dipping sauce.

Heat a splash of sunflower oil in a heavy-based frying pan (skillet), then carefully place the stuffed flowers into the pan (you may need to cook in batches). Turn after a minute, or when it starts to become golden, and cook until golden all over.

Serve hot or at room temperature with a bowl of the dipping sauce (discard the stems as you eat).

Hoba Miso Beef

Hoba (magnolia leaf) miso is a regional speciality from Japan. The rehydrated dried leaves add a fragrant scent to the food. Eating magnolia leaves originates from when fresh vegetables were scarce during long, cold winters, but now they're eaten as a delicacy. This dish is traditionally cooked over embers but also works in a hot pan.

SERVES 4

8 large magnolia leaves, dried or fresh
4 tbsp brown miso paste
2 tbsp mirin
2 tsp sugar
300 g (10½ oz) marbled beef steak, thinly sliced
4 shiitake mushrooms (can substitute for portobello mushrooms), thinly sliced
1 spring onion (scallion), finely chopped

Soak the magnolia leaves in water for 20 minutes.

Meanwhile, heat a barbecue or a heavy-based pan until hot. Mix together the miso, mirin and sugar in a bowl.

Remove the soaked magnolia leaves from the water and pat them dry with paper towels. Spread one side of each leaf with a generous layer of the miso mixture; place the leaves onto a hot pan or grill (the miso facing up) and place the mushrooms and beef strips on top of the miso, dividing them equally. When the miso starts to sizzle, turn the heat to its lowest setting. Cook until the beef is browned on both sides, turning as needed.

Remove from the heat, scatter with spring onion and serve with rice.

Magnolia Spice

Magnolia petals transform as they dry from white, pink and creamy shades to dark brown, which is due to the petals oxidising as they warm. The same effect happens on cold nights when the flowers in full bloom can be hit by hard frosts, leaving you to wake to a tree that has turned from a showy display of light to one like falling autumn leaves. Fortunately, the flavour is not lost when your petals are frost damaged, so head out in the morning to gather up the browning flowers. Lay them on a dehydrating tray or on a piece of baking parchment and dry. Magnolia petals are full of water so they will take a longer time than other petals to dry out, and they need to be laid out singly rather than overlapping to dry properly.

Magnolia spice is wonderful when added to sweet buns like hot cross buns – add a couple of ground teaspoons to the dough, in place of mixed spice.

MAKES 150 g (5½ oz) jar

When your petals (approx. 30 flower heads' worth) have dried and turned papery brown, place them in a spice grinder and blend to a powder. Spoon into a jar and label as magnolia ginger powder, because that is what you will have: a flower petal that tastes like ground ginger. Use for anything you would use ginger in: biscuits, cakes, puddings, gingerbread, soups, curries or casseroles.

MAKES 1 × 500 ML (17 FL OZ) JAR

Pickled Magnolia Flowers

Magnolia petals not only mimic dried ginger as a powdered spice, but also cleverly assume a very convincing impression of thinly sliced pickled ginger in sushi, stir fries, ramen noodle soups or even salads.

200 g (7 oz) magnolia petals, washed
400 ml (14 fl oz/generous 1½ cups) rice wine vinegar
50 g (1¾ oz/¼ cup) unrefined sugar
generous pinch of salt

OPTIONAL EXTRAS

a couple of garlic cloves
lime zest
a few Sichuan peppercorns
a few cardamom pods

Pack a 500 ml (17 fl oz) jar with the magnolia petals.

Heat the vinegar, sugar, salt and any chosen flavouring, if using, in a saucepan until the sugar has dissolved. Leave to cool slightly (if the vinegar is scorching it will cook the petals).

Pour the vinegar mixture over the petals, making sure they are fully submerged. Seal the lid and turn upside down as it cools (to help sterilise the lid). Leave the pickle to mature overnight before using.

Since rice wine vinegar is a low acidic vinegar it doesn't act as a long-term preservative, so these pickles are best eaten within a few weeks. If you would like to keep your pickled flowers for longer, substitute the rice wine vinegar with apple cider vinegar.

SERVES 4

Miso Aubergine with Magnolia Leaves

Magnolia leaves infuse a unique flavour into food, the younger leaves have an almost citrus scent. Stuffed between slices of aubergine (eggplant) that have been coated in a salty miso paste, the magnolia leaves infuse their perfume into the flesh of the vegetable to create a collapsingly soft, umami-rich dish.

- 4 tbsp miso (white or dark)
- 3 tbsp honey
- 4 tbsp olive oil
- 2 tbsp rice vinegar
- pinch of salt, if needed
- 2 large aubergines (eggplants)
- 20 magnolia leaves
- sesame seeds, for sprinkling
- chives, finely chopped, for sprinkling

Preheat the oven to 190°C (375°F/gas 5).

In a large bowl, mix together the miso, honey, oil and vinegar. Since the miso is salty, taste the mixture and only add salt if needed.

Cut the aubergines lengthways into eight wedges and immediately place in the bowl with the sauce, coating all sides of the aubergine. Place half the magnolia leaves on the bottom of the baking dish, placing the aubergine on top, with the remaining leaves sandwiched between each wedge. Keep any remaining sauce to baste the aubergines with during cooking.

Roast in the oven for 20 minutes, then remove, baste with more sauce and sprinkle with sesame seeds. Put the dish back in the oven and roast for another 15 minutes until the edges of the aubergines start to darken and crisp. Remove any burnt leaves before serving the dish either hot or at room temperature with rice and a sprinkling of chives and sesame seeds.

FLAVOUR PROFILE Sweet · Buttery · Apple · Lemon (the leaves can be bitter as they age).

Primrose

COMMONLY USED EDIBLE SPECIES

Primula vulgaris (common primrose).

WHERE THEY GROW

Primrose thrives in partial shade, but will grow in full sun and prefers moist soil, ideally slightly acidic.

WHEN TO GATHER

Late winter to late spring – the leaves can be collected until they wilt in the summer.

Of all the wild plants that grow beyond the manicured confines of gardens, the common primrose is one of the few that people purposely bring back with them to plant. Even when it arrives unexpectedly, and starts spreading clumps of less-than-beautiful, tongue-shaped leaves, it's not seen as a weed, rather a welcome addition. Is it because the flowers are lovelier than others? Not quite – it's no more radiant than a buttercup or dandelion and these plants are treated with disdain by people who like orderly plots. Perhaps it's because primroses don't spread out of control? But that's not right either because one primrose will quickly multiply through the garden. Perhaps it's more to do with the fact that it comes into flower when most other plants – wild or tamed – are still deep underground, dormant in the late-winter chill. Primroses fill the cold bare earth with their clumps of green leaves and warm sunshine yellow colour as the *prima rose* (first flower) of the year.

PARTS USED

① Flowers
② Leaves (roots medicinally)

CAUTION

Primroses contain salicylic acids, which should be used with caution if you are on blood thinners or pregnant. If using the leaves, take great care not to mistake fatally toxic foxgloves for primrose leaves. Collecting from the plant when it is still in flower helps to make sure you have the correct plant.

Whatever the reason behind why we grow them in our tended beds now, the first primroses to be brought into our gardens were placed there more for their functional uses than their beauty. For most people in the Middle Ages, gardens were about providing food and medicine, and it was as both that primroses were prized. They were infused into sauces, vinegars, salads and puddings, (including a very regal dessert made with ground almonds and honey – the petals used as adornments), but their medicinal prowess was also valued.

For as long as such records were kept, primroses have been part of the pantheon of healing plants. In the Roman Empire, Pliny viewed the little plant as a cure-all for ailments ranging from rheumatism and delirium to gout, and ever since then (and probably for a long time beforehand) primroses were praised for their medicinal properties. Rich in saponins and glycosides, they soothe muscular aches and pains, ease headaches, clear skin conditions, heal wounds, itching eyes, coughs and even calm stress. Unlike other plants, primroses didn't fall out of fashion in the medicinal world – it's as popular today as it ever was. Unfortunately for the primrose, its most valuable medical asset is in its roots, which have the largest amounts of the in-demand compounds, and so every year vast amounts of wild primrose plants are dug up – ending up in the tablets we take for our aches and pains. As our global population explodes, so demand for medicines grows as well, and huge amounts of primroses are uprooted, never to flower again. This harvesting, accompanied with a loss of habitat and changing climate, has turned the common primrose into a rarity in the parts of the world where it once grew in abundance.

Fortunately, there is one environment where the plant is nurtured and healthy: our gardens. Because now that we grow them for that beautiful burst of spring colour, rather than for their roots, gardeners have become the custodian of the plant – its domesticated habitat has become its sanctuary. If you have primroses in your garden, care for them. If you don't have any yet, plant a couple of clumps and in a few years they'll dot across the ground, and repay you not only with longed-for colour, but a sustainable, delicious and beneficial crop. Harvesting the leaves and flowers from your growing population also encourages new flowers to grow, because as all gardeners know, one of the keys to continual flowering is deadheading (straight into your kitchen).

Should you not yet have swathes of plants lining your garden paths and only have a handful of flowers to use, as you deadhead, freeze the flowers in a container until you accumulate enough to turn into your desired treat. Of course, you could always turn the primroses into candied jewels to adorn a cake – as a thank you from the flowers for giving them a place to grow.

SERVES 4 (AND MAKES 350 ML [12 FL OZ/ SCANT 1½ CUPS] PRIMROSE VINEGAR)

Asparagus Primrosa

Asparagus spears start emerging from the soil as primroses are at the height of flowering. The lemony, almost buttery flavour of the flowers makes a delicious dressing flecked with sunshine yellow for this celebration of the best of the vibrant flavours of spring.

1 tbsp primrose-infused white wine vinegar (see below)
1 tsp honey
1 tsp wholegrain or Dijon mustard
3 tbsp light olive oil
1 small shallot, finely chopped
1 tbsp capers, finely chopped
handful of fresh primrose flowers and small leaves
1 bunch of asparagus spears
salt and black pepper, to taste

TO MAKE THE VINEGAR

500ml (17 fl oz/generous 2 cups) jug full of primrose flowers
350ml (11¼ fl oz/1⅓ cups) white wine vinegar

To make the primrose-infused vinegar, blend the primrose flowers with the white wine vinegar. Once the flowers have been puréed into the vinegar, leave them to infuse for 24 hours before straining out and bottling the infused vinegar.

Prepare the dressing by whisking together the infused vinegar, honey, mustard and olive oil until emulsified. Stir through the shallot and capers. Coarsely chop half of the primrose flowers and stir into the dressing. Leave the vinaigrette to macerate for 30 minutes. Season with salt and pepper.

Snap the woody ends off the asparagus (you can use these in soups). Steam the tender stems for 5 minutes or until just starting to become tender, then drain and place on a serving platter. Spoon the vinaigrette over the asparagus spears and toss until well covered. Coarsely chop or pull apart the remaining primrose flowers and finely slice the leaves into grass-like slivers, then scatter over the dressed asparagus.

Serve as a simple but delicious starter, or with a boiled egg as a light lunch.

Crab and Primrose Linguine

Crabs come into season in the middle of spring when primroses are at their most profuse. Celebrate the return of warming waters and weather with a meal that lemony primroses elevate and will make the most weather-beaten of fishermen feel a warm glow.

SERVES 4

500 g (1 lb 2 oz) linguine
3 tbsp olive oil
1 garlic clove, finely chopped
1 small red chilli, deseeded and finely chopped
1 small glass white wine
100 g (3½ oz) brown and white crab meat
½ cup finely chopped parsley
½ cup primrose petals pulled from the flower head
4–5 large, tender primrose leaves, finely sliced into slivers
zest of 1 lemon
salt, to taste

Cook the pasta according to the packet instructions until al dente (usually around 9–10 minutes).

While the pasta cooks, heat the oil in a large pan (one that is large enough to eventually hold the pasta) over a medium heat, add the garlic and chilli, and cook for a few seconds before pouring over the white wine. Simmer for a few minutes before adding half of the crab meat (if you have separate brown and white meat, add the brown meat at this stage). When the pasta is al dente, add it to the pan and stir until covered in sauce. Remove from the heat and taste before seasoning with salt.

Serve immediately, scattered with the remaining crab meat, the chopped parsley, primrose flowers and leaves, and a few gratings of lemon zest.

Primrose-and-Herb-Coated Goat's Cheese

The buttery yellow of primroses set against new vibrant green growth almost encapsulates the essence of spring in two colours. You'd be hard-pressed to make a morsel that better represented the vibrancy of spring than this fresh-as-a-daisy soft goat's cheese rolled in green dill, sour sorrel, chives and yellow primrose petals. Serve with crackers and a glass of wine and soak up the spring season.

SERVES 4
(as a side dish or as part of a cheese platter)

1 small bunch of sorrel leaves (if you don't have sorrel you can use zest of ½ lemon)
1 small bunch of chives
1 small bunch of dill
1 small bunch of primrose flowers (about 20 flowers)
2 small goat's cheese logs

If you want to prepare this dish in advance, swap the sorrel for lemon zest, as sorrel can discolour when cut.

Very finely chop the herbs and primrose flowers into flecks and scatter evenly over a piece of greaseproof paper that is wider than the circumference of the goat's cheese logs. Place each goat's cheese log on one end of the herb-covered paper and roll across, pressing the cheese into the herbs so that they stick well (if the cheese has a very dry coating, dampen the outside with water to make it more likely to pick up the herbs). Roll the paper around the cheeses, and place in the refrigerator until you are ready to serve.

SERVES 4

Primrose Leaf Tempura

Primrose leaves are robust enough to hold their form when deep-fried in tempura batter. Their slightly lemony flavour makes them a perfect leaf to batter and plunge into soy dipping sauces. Tempura'd leaves are best eaten as soon as you make them, so make the sauce first and fight for the crispy leaves as they come out of the frying pan.

60 g (2 oz/½ cup) plain (all-purpose) flour
1 tbsp rice flour
½ tsp baking powder
100–120 ml (3½–4 fl oz/scant ½–½ cup) water
1 ice cube
vegetable oil, for deep-frying
20 primrose leaves

FOR THE DIPPING SAUCE

250 ml (8 fl oz/1 cup) dashi soup stock
60 ml (2 fl oz/¼ cup) mirin
60 ml (2 fl oz/¼ cup) light soy sauce
1½ tsp sugar
thumb-sized piece of daikon or radish
primrose flowers, finely sliced, to garnish (optional)

Make the dipping sauce by heating the dashi, mirin, soy sauce and sugar in a saucepan until the sugar has dissolved and the sauce has slightly reduced. Transfer to a serving dish, grate over the daikon or radish and add the flowers for decoration. Set aside.

Put the dry ingredients in a bowl and stir them well to ensure the ingredients are thoroughly blended. Make a well in the middle and pour in the water, whisking the liquid into a batter. Add the ice cube to chill the batter down.

Meanwhile, heat a 5 cm (2 in) depth of vegetable oil in a deep pan until it is sizzling hot (you can test by dropping a small piece of bread into the oil; it is ready when it sizzles and rises to the surface). When the oil is ready, dip your primrose leaves in the batter – you can either press just one side into the batter to show off the leaf when it is cooked or fully cover each one. Carefully lower the battered primrose leaves onto the oil and cook until golden.

Remove with a slotted spoon to paper towels to absorb any excess oil and eat immediately, dipped into the sauce.

MAKES 20

Crystallised Primrose Flowers

Sweet edible flowers, including roses, violets, carnations and lilacs, have a long history of being crystallised and primrose flowers are amongst the most prized to preserve like this. Traditionally, flowers were coated in gum arabic – a paste made from resin collected from the acacia tree. You can still buy gum arabic, but if you use it make sure that you buy a food-grade product (gum arabic is also used as an artists' ingredient).

- 20 primrose flowers, collected with stems attached
- 1 egg white, lightly beaten (or a gum arabic paste made by dissolving 1 part gum arabic powder into 3 parts just-boiled water)
- 115 g (3¾ oz/½ cup) caster (superfine) sugar, ground to a powder

Plunge the primrose flowers into a bowl of cold water and gently agitate the water to make sure that any dirt comes away from the flowers. Scoop the flowers out of the bowl and drain in a colander before drying in a salad spinner.

Line a cooling rack with greaseproof paper and use tape to stick the paper to the rack, making sure the paper is taut. Use a skewer to poke stem-sized holes into the paper – you'll need as many holes as you have flowers. Holding each flower by its stem, use a clean fine paintbrush to paint the entire surface of each flower with the egg white (or gum arabic paste), remembering to paint the top of the stems as well. Sift the powdered sugar on the bottom of each flower, then poke each stem into the holes in the paper so that the petals don't rest on the surface. Dust the remaining sugar over the top of the flowers, making sure to cover the whole flower. Leave in a warm place to dry, and store in an airtight container. If you have more petals than will cover one layer, use a piece of greaseproof paper between each layer to stop them from sticking to each other.

Use to decorate cakes and desserts or as a garnish on cocktails. Crystallised flowers also make a special date-marking gift for anniversaries or weddings.

SERVES 6

Primrose Curd Meringues

Primrose flowers' hint of buttery lemon flavour makes them a dream ingredient in desserts that glow with the promise of spring. You can make this as individual meringues, fit for high teas in the garden, or as one large pavlova for a spring feast.

FOR THE PRIMROSE CURD

- 500 ml (17 fl oz/generous 2 cups) jug of primrose flowers
- 225 g (8 oz/1 cup) granulated sugar
- 225 g (8 oz) Bramley apples
- zest and juice of 1 lemon
- 125 g (4 oz) unsalted butter
- 2 large eggs

FOR THE MERINGUE

- 4 large egg whites
- 240 g (8½ oz/generous 1 cup) caster (superfine) sugar

TO SERVE

- 150 ml (5 fl oz/scant ⅔ cup) double (heavy) cream, whipped
- extra primrose flowers
- lemon zest

Start by making the primrose curd. Place the flowers and sugar in a food processor and lightly blend until the primrose flowers start to break up and the sugar looks damp. Spoon the mixture into a bowl and leave at room temperature for a few hours or overnight (this will allow the flavours from the petals to infuse the sugar).

When the sugar is ready, peel, core and chop the apples. Place the chopped apples into a pan with the lemon zest and 100 ml (3½ fl oz/scant ½ cup) water, and gently cook until the apple is soft. Let cool, then blend into a smooth purée.

Half fill a pan with water and place a snug-fitting heatproof bowl on top. Add the apple purée, lemon juice, butter and primrose sugar to the bowl. Slowly heat, stirring the mixture until the butter has completely melted and the sugar has dissolved. Turn off the heat and let the mixture cool slightly.

Beat the eggs in a cup, then slowly pour them through a sieve into the curd mixture, stirring thoroughly with a balloon whisk until the eggs are completely incorporated. Put the pan back on a gentle heat and stir the mixture for about 10 minutes until it thickens (it will thicken further as it cools).

Pour the curd into sterilised jars, seal immediately and store in the refrigerator, where it will keep for up to 1 month.

To make the meringues, preheat the oven to 120°C (250°F/gas ½). Line a large baking sheet with non-stick baking parchment.

Put the egg whites and about a quarter of the sugar in a large bowl and whisk to soft peaks. Still whisking, gradually sprinkle in all but about 3 tablespoons of the sugar, beating until it is holding soft peaks again. Finally, fold in the last of the sugar.

Spoon the mixture onto the prepared baking sheet in 20 mounds spaced about 3cm (1¼ in) apart, or create one large pavlova base. Bake for 1 hour, or until dry and firm to the touch (it will take longer to bake if you are making a large meringue). Leave to cool on the paper.

Very carefully peel the meringues from the paper and place on a plate with a spoonful of the curd and a dollop of whipped cream. Decorate with primrose flowers and lemon zest.

FLAVOUR PROFILE Floral · Herbal · Fruity.

Flowering Currant

COMMONLY USED EDIBLE SPECIES

Ribes sanguineum (red flowering currant).

WHERE THEY GROW

Flowering currants grow best in full sun to partial shade, in well-drained soils.

WHEN TO GATHER

Flowers — late winter to mid-spring

Leaves — until late summer/autumn (fall)

The moment that winter and spring brush against each other, when most other deciduous plant leaves are still tightly in bud, hiding from the frost, the flowering currant shrub bursts into life, covered with vibrant pink clusters of little blooms that hang like grapes, filling the warming air with their sweet, fruity perfume.

PARTS USED

① Flowers
② Leaves
③ Fruits

In the shrub's native homeland of the west coast of America, its berries are one of many species of currant that have been a part of human diets for thousands of years. If you've ever eaten the fruit of a flowering currant, you'll know that it's rather inferior to its deliciously sour siblings: black, white and red currant. And, unsurprisingly, where it is eaten, it's often mixed with other fruits rather than consumed by itself.

In the 18th century, the beautiful (if blandly fruited) shrub was collected by British botanist David Douglas, who had been sent by the Royal Horticultural Society to the Pacific Northwest of America to find new plant species with which to fill the flower beds of Europe. Flowering currant was an immediate success, as it provided that elusive early burst of colour for gardens, and it was quickly spread by gardeners across Europe – its forgettable berries disregarded and left for the birds.

However, flowering currant wasn't entirely ignored as a plant to eat – the incredibly scented early blooms replaced the fruit as its go-to part to consume. Not forgetting its leaves, which have an aromatic, almost rose- and sage-like flavour, and which also turn their hand to being a rather lovely herbal flavouring.

There may be a few of you reading this who are feeling incredibly sceptical about flowering currant tasting good, because whilst most people standing near one of the shrubs smell a heady mix of rose, sage, thyme and currants, you might smell something very different indeed – a smell that is best not described in a cookery book – a smell only a few can detect, which might also mean you recoil at the scent of elderflowers in full bloom. This smell, a cunning defence mechanism to make delicious flowers less desirable is made by a ketone chemical, which is released when the plants are under stress. It increases if a stem has been picked, to the point that most of us non-super-smellers can eventually detect its distinctive odour (for instance, if you leave a bowl of elderflowers, or indeed flowering currant, out for too long in your kitchen). To avoid discovering what this smell is like, use your flowers as soon as you pick them – even drying or freezing will halt it from developing. If you are one of the unfortunate souls for whom flowering currant smells less than delicious, then step back from this section of the book, because unlike its bland fruits, you'll not be able to make it taste better no matter how many other flavours you blend the flowers with.

For the rest of us lucky non-ketone smellers, treasure awaits. Harvest the flowers as soon as they open. This will give you the sweetest, most floral flavour, because for most of us these flowers taste as they smell: fruity, floral and herbal. You can simply scatter them onto salads, cakes and even into tagines, or on roast fatty meats, oily fish and buttery sauces. If you want to preserve the flavour of flowering currant, steep them into vinegars and syrups. They'll even store for a few months in sealed containers in the freezer – especially handy if you want to enjoy them in cooling ice creams or sorbets when the weather has warmed up. Just remember to check with anyone you plan to give it to what they make of flowering currant bushes – you'll know by their response whether they'll thank or curse you for serving it to them.

SERVES 4

Smoked Mackerel and Flowering Currant Pâté with Apple and Rhubarb Salsa

Flowering currants bloom at the peak of the forced rhubarb season, bright pink bedfellows that inject longed-for colour and fruity flavours into early spring diets. Both rhubarb and flowering currants are delicious served with smoked mackerel pâté, cutting through the rich oiliness. Serve on big floury rolls or toast as a light lunch.

2 whole smoked mackerel fillets, skinned
2 tsp horseradish sauce
2 tbsp crème fraîche
juice of 1 lemon
10 flowering currant flower heads, pulled apart into individual flowers
1 rhubarb stalk
1 firm apple
1 shallot
1 small bunch of dill and/or chervil
4 white rolls or 8 slices of toast
salt and black pepper, to taste

To make the pâté, place the mackerel in a blender with the horseradish, crème fraîche, half the lemon juice and a good grinding of black pepper. Blend to a rough paste, then add most of the currant flowers (reserve a few for garnish) and pulse to combine. Season with salt to taste and chill until needed.

Finely dice the rhubarb, apple and shallot, place them all in a bowl and immediately stir through the remaining lemon juice. Chop most of the herbs (reserving a few leaves for garnish) and stir into the fruit and shallot mixture.

Spread the pâté onto the bread or toast, top with the salsa and sprinkle over the reserved currant flowers and remaining herb leaves pulled into small pieces.

SERVES 4 AS A STARTER, 2 AS A MAIN COURSE

Gnocchi with Flowering Currant Leaf Butter

Flowering currant leaves are an often overlooked part of the plant, but with wisps of lemon and sage they make a beautiful herb to cut through the fat of dishes such as this brown-buttered gnocchi.

500 g (1 lb 2 oz) gnocchi
50 g (1¾ oz) unsalted butter
8 flowering currant leaves, finely chopped into grass-like slivers
1 tbsp olive oil
finely grated zest of 1 lemon (about ½ tsp)
20 g (¾ oz) Parmesan
salt, to taste
bread, to serve

Bring a pan of salted water to the boil. When the water is vigorously boiling, drop in the gnocchi dumplings. After a couple of minutes, they'll float to the surface – leave them cooking for 30 seconds after they float to the top before scooping them out of the water and draining (you can lay the dumplings on an absorbent cloth to help them dry).

While the gnocchi are drying, make the flavoured brown butter. Cut the butter into small pieces and place in a saucepan – ideally use a light-coloured pan so that you can see when the butter is browning. Whisk the butter over a low heat until it starts turning brown. If you have a lot of impurities building up in the pan, pour the melted butter through a metal sieve into a jug. Season with salt, add most of the flowering currant leaves (reserve some for garnish) and set aside.

Wipe the pan clean and put back on the heat. Add the olive oil and, once sizzling hot, add the drained gnocchi and brown until the undersides are golden and crisp. Turn the dumplings over and fry the other sides until crispy, then pour over the browned butter. Stir to coat the dumplings for 30 seconds, then spoon into serving bowls.

Garnish with the reserved flowering currant leaves and a few sprinkles of lemon zest, and grate over some Parmesan just before serving. Serve immediately with chunks of bread to mop up any buttery sauce that evades the gnocchi (gnocchi is best eaten as soon as it is cooked).

SERVES 4–6

Flowering Currant and Apple Sauce

Apple sauce is a perfect foil to rich meats like pork. The floral and sage flavours of the flowers not only make it taste more vibrant but also add beautiful flecks of colour to a traditional roast.

1 kg (2 lb 4 oz) Bramley apples
juice of 1 lemon
4 tbsp water
2 tbsp granulated sugar
60 g (2 oz) butter
½ cup flowering currant petals pulled from the main flower head
salt, to taste (optional)

Peel, core and dice the apples (if you have freezer space, save the peels and cores in a bag until you have enough to cook into apple pectin – see page 128 for the recipe). Place the apples in a pan with the lemon juice, water and sugar, and cook gently over a low heat until the apple collapses. Keep stirring the pan while the apple is cooking to make sure that nothing on the bottom of the pan catches and burns.

Once the apple has completely softened, stir in the butter and purée the apple by pressing with the back of a spoon (if you want a smoother sauce, pass it through a sieve). Stir in the flowering currant petals and leave to infuse for 10 minutes before tasting and seasoning with a pinch of salt if required.

MAKES A 20 CM (8 IN) CAKE

Flowering Currant and Honey Polenta Cake

Flowering currants are delicious infused into sweet cordials, syrup and honey – the flowers' strong flavour is a perfect match for the equally domineering taste of honey. Make a jar of infused honey by warming 300 ml (10 fl oz/1¼ cups) honey in a pan over a low heat until it is very liquid. Add a couple of handfuls of flowering currant flowers to the honey, stir and leave over a very low heat to infuse for a couple of hours before straining. You can use this honey to sweeten herbal teas or as a floral honey for bread and butter.

FOR THE CAKE

- 100 g (3½ oz/generous ¾ cup) self-raising flour
- 130 g (4 oz/scant 1 cup) polenta
- 100 ml (3½ fl oz/scant ½ cup) light olive oil
- 100 g (3½ oz/generous ⅓ cup) Greek yoghurt, plus extra to serve
- 200 ml (7 fl oz/scant 1 cup) honey infused with flowering currant (see recipe introduction)
- 3 eggs
- 2 tbsp orange juice
- a few flowering currant flowers, to decorate

FOR THE SYRUP

- 60 ml (2 fl oz/¼ cup) orange juice
- 3 tbsp honey infused with flowering currant (see recipe introduction)

Preheat the oven to 180°C (350°F/gas 4). Line a 20 cm (8 in) cake tin (pan) with baking parchment.

Mix all the cake ingredients, except the flowers for decoration, together in a bowl until you have a smooth batter. Pour the batter into the prepared cake tin, cover with an ovenproof plate and bake for 35 minutes (removing the plate after 15 minutes) or until an inserted skewer in the middle of the cake comes out clean.

To make the syrup, warm the orange juice in a small pan and stir in the infused honey.

Remove the cake from the oven and leave to cool for a few minutes, then prick holes into the top of the cake with a skewer and pour the syrup over. Allow the syrup to soak into the cake before serving.

Serve as a dessert with Greek yoghurt, scattered with a few extra flowering currant flowers to decorate.

SERVES 6

Flowering Currant Sorbet

Flowering currant blooms can be frozen in tubs until you need to use them, which is handy for this ice-cold sorbet that likes to be eaten on the warmer days of spring rather than the icy chill that the early flowers can open to. Flowering currant season may have the misfortune of coming at a time of year when the weather flip flops between winter and summer on an almost daily basis, but it is also in season at the same time as citrus fruits are at their peak; the perfect excuse to fill yellow lemon shells with the bright pink sorbet.

- 1 litre (34 fl oz/4¼ cups) jug of flowering currant flowers
- 300 ml (10 fl oz/1¼ cups) just-boiled water (cooled slightly so it doesn't scald the flowers)
- 4 large unwaxed lemons
- 150 g (5½ oz/scant ¾ cup) granulated sugar
- 1 tbsp liquid glucose

Make a flowering currant tea by pouring the hot water over most of the flowers in a heatproof bowl (reserve a handful for later). Cover and leave to infuse until the flowers have become pale and the liquid a dull mauve colour. Strain, squeezing any remaining liquid from the flowers before discarding them.

Slice three of the lemons in half along their sides and cut the bottoms flat so that the shells can sit on a plate. With a small knife, carefully cut out the flesh. Blitz the lemon flesh in a blender and sieve the juice. Place the empty lemon shells in a freezerproof container and freeze.

Combine the sugar and lemon zest from the fourth lemon with 100 ml (3½ fl oz/scant ½ cup) water in a saucepan and heat until the sugar dissolves. Remove from the heat and stir in 150 ml (5 fl oz/scant ⅔ cup) of the flowering currant liquid and the reserved lemon juice (at this point the liquid will turn bright pink). Leave to cool, then pour into a large freezerproof container and freeze until solid (if you don't have a large container, divide the mixture between two).

Tip the iced mixture out onto a board (you might need to run it under boiled water to release it). Using a bread knife, cut (or smash) the ice block into chunks, place in a food processor and blend until it is broken up like a granita. Pour in the liquid glucose and blend again until the mixture is pale and smooth. Crumble in the reserved currant flowers, then pour back into the freezer-proof container and place back in the freezer for a couple of hours to firm up before scooping into the frozen lemon shells. Place the filled lemons into sealed containers and freeze until ready to serve (they will keep for a couple of weeks).

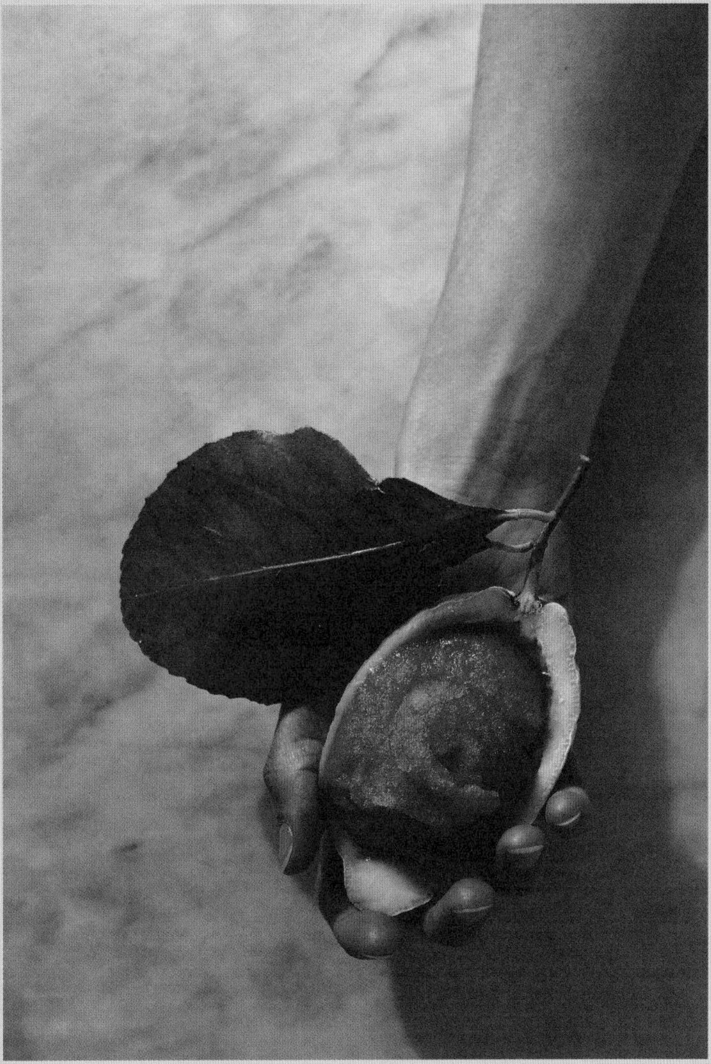

FLAVOUR PROFILE

CHERRY BLOSSOM is floral, slightly bitter with an almond flavour that intensifies when cooked or soaked in salt. The leaves have a more intense almond / vanilla flavour.

CHERRY FRUITS range from sweet to incredibly sour and bitter.

Cherry

COMMONLY USED EDIBLE SPECIES

For blossoms – *Prunus x yedoensis* (Yoshino cherry)

For leaves – *Prunus speciosa* (Oshima cherry)

For fruit – *Prunus cerasus* (sour cherry), *Prunus serotina* (black cherry), *Prunus avium* (wild cherry), *Prunus avium* Bing (Bing cherry)

WHERE THEY GROW

Cherry trees thrive in sheltered spots in well-drained, deep, fertile soil, especially if the soil is slightly acidic.

WHEN TO GATHER

Flower buds, flowers and newly-opened leaves – spring

Fruit and leaves – summer

In Japan, meteorologists don't just predict the weather, but something else that transfixes people even more than whether it's going to rain or not. Each year, the Japanese Meteorological Corporation forecasts the coming cherry blossom season, predicting the blossoming of trees across over 1,000 locations across the country. Hanami (the cherry blossom gazing festival) is one of the highlights of Japan's cultural calendar and attracts millions of people who sit and picnic under the flowering trees, chasing the blooms as they open across the country.

PARTS USED

① Flowers
② Leaves
③ Fruits

CAUTION

Whilst all cherries are edible, not all species have edible leaves and flowers; check your species before you use them and don't use wilted leaves or flowers, or any that have been sprayed with insecticide.

Be aware that cherry leaves, blossoms and twigs are poisonous to some domestic animals.

Watching cherry blossoms opening isn't just a practice from the age of television weather forecasters, but one that goes far back in history, all the way to 700 AD when Japanese envoys to China first saw their sophisticated neighbours celebrate the flowering of plum trees with food and poetry readings. The envoys returned to Japan with aspirations to do the same. As with most new fashions, the cherry blossom gazing events were at first elite affairs but swiftly spread across the country as a national festival. Cherries were already revered in Japan as the opening of the blossoms was thought to be associated with the arrival of the goddess of the Fuji Mountains, who came down from the hills as it was time to plant new rice seeds. Cherry blossoms are to this day known as *sakura* in Japan, *sa* meaning 'the god of rice' and *kura* meaning an 'altar', since – as all gods should have – offerings of flowers and sake were left for her on altars in the early spring.

These days, you're more likely to find the word *sakura* on menus, referring to little salty preserved flowers, which are used to lace all kinds of food during the blossom-watching season and beyond. Salting the flowers not only helps preserve them at their peak when the buds are about to open, but helps them develop incredible flavours of vanilla and almond. The salty almondy flowers can be infused into sweet dishes like mochi, macarons, ice cream and milk puddings, and also into savoury dishes such as *natto* (fermented soybeans), udon noodles and sushi.

It's not just the blossoms that hide delicious flavours, young cherry leaves also have a similar taste. They may not be as flamboyant as the flowers but they are just as lovely in taste.

Eating cherry blossoms may be associated with Japan, but cherry trees and all of their edible parts have a far wider reach. The original cherry trees were thought to originate in Asia Minor, where unlike in Japan they are grown less for their showy blooms and more for their sour fruit, and the kernels inside their pits. These are processed to make them safe to eat and ground into a powder called *mahlab*, which is used as a sweet spice in everything from yeasted breads to sweets, milk puddings and drinks – even meatballs flavoured with cherry sauces benefit from a pinch of the spice.

If you visit Anatolia, the home of the cherry, you'll find a cuisine that loves to wrap food in leaves – vine leaves, mulberry leaves and cherry leaves. Just like vine leaves, cherry leaves are collected when they are tender and young, blanched and preserved in brine or frozen until they are made into dishes like *Kiraz Yapragı Sarması*, tiny, pencil-thin wraps that are filled with burghul wheat, and cooked in sweet or savoury sauces.

The taste of infused cherry leaves is not lost on liqueur-loving European drink makers either. In France, cherry leaves are macerated in red wine, vodka and sugar to make regional specialities such as *vin de cerises* and *Guignloet de Dijon*; and, in Italy, *100 Foglie di Romagna*. The perfect tipple to appreciate a cherry tree in blossom or just in leaf.

Before you go and gorge on cherry leaves, flowers and kernels, be aware that their beautiful flavours are created by a chemical called amygdalin. Amygdalin is found in lots of foods, but is in higher quantities in certain fruits (it's especially high in bitter almond kernels) and when crushed, amygdalin reacts with another compound to create cyanide compounds. So, avoid eating raw, unprocessed cherry kernels and whilst there's only a small amount of the chemical in cherry leaves and flowers, it's best to use them in moderation or to cook them (heat and other processes make the chemical inert). If you're not cooking the leaves, use them to infuse flavour rather than to eat.

SERVES 4

Lamb Meatballs with Sour Cherry Sauce

All cherry trees produce edible fruit. You might find, however, that the most lovely blossoming trees produce super sour, bitter cherries. You'll probably not want to put them in your fruit bowl, but sour cherries are an ingredient not to pass by; when cooked, they transform into luxurious cherry pie fillings and make incredible sour sauces for savoury food such as cherry molasses and this Anatolian-inspired dish of lamb with sour cherry sauce, flavoured with a blend of spices called baharat. Originally from the Levant, but fortunately now available in shops across the world, baharat is an aromatic, warming blend that can be used as a dry rub on meats, for braised vegetables, in soups or as a condiment.

FOR THE MEATBALLS

1 small onion, roughly chopped
250 g (9 oz) minced (ground) lamb
1 scant tsp baharat spice blend
½ tsp ground cinnamon
½ tsp salt

FOR THE SOUR CHERRY SAUCE

500 g (1 lb 2 oz/2½ cups) pitted sour cherries
50 g (1¾ oz/¼ cup) caster (superfine) sugar
½ tsp ground cinnamon
½ tsp salt

TO SERVE

25g (¾ oz) pine nuts
1 bunch of parsley, chopped
pita breads

Preheat the oven to 180°C (350°F/gas 4).

Place the onion in a food processor and blitz to a purée, then add the lamb, baharat spice blend, cinnamon and salt. Blitz until well combined. Divide and roll the meat paste into walnut-sized balls, place on a baking sheet and bake for 10 minutes.

Meanwhile, blend 400g (14 oz/2 cups) of the sour cherries in the cleaned food processor, then strain, collecting the juices in a saucepan. Add the sugar, cinnamon and salt, bring to the boil over a medium heat, then reduce to a gentle simmer until the sauce starts to thicken.

Add the meatballs and remaining sour cherries to the sauce and cook until everything is well heated through.

Spoon into a serving dish, scatter with pine nuts and chopped parsley and serve with pita breads.

MAKES A 200 G (7 OZ) JAR

Sakura – Salted Cherry Blossoms or Leaves

Sakura is both a term used to describe cherry blossoms and the preserves made with the blossoms and leaves. Some *sakuras* are made by pickling the blossoms in vinegar, others by simply brining them in salt. This process allows for the development of their delicious flavours.

You can use any kind of edible cherry blossom to make into *sakura*, but blossoms from ornamental cherry trees with pink double flowers are the most prized. These trees are known as *yaezakura* and are commonly found in urban streets and parks. Choose blossoms that are just starting to open, and young leaves that are as tender as possible (you can still use fully open flowers, but they'll not hold together as well and the petals are more liable to falling off the stems).

Once you've made your preserve with salty, almond flavours, you can use it in a wide range of recipes: *sakura manju* (sweet yeasted buns with finely chopped flowers through the dough); *sakura senbei* (toasted rice crackers with salted leaves); *sakura yokan* (a set jelly); in Japan *sakura* is even used to flavour seasonal KitKats and Oreo biscuits. The sky is the blossoming limit.

- 50 g (1¾ oz) cherry blossoms or leaves, rinsed
- 2 tsp sea salt, plus extra as needed

If using blossoms, place them in a bowl or plastic container and sprinkle with the salt. Toss the blossoms in the salt to make sure they are fully covered. Refrigerate for a couple of days. A brine liquid will start to seep out into the bottom of the container.

Remove the blossoms from the brine and lay on a tray on a piece of baking parchment. Place somewhere warm (a very low oven would work) until they have dried out. Sprinkle with more salt before storing in an airtight jar. Soak for a few minutes in water before using.

If you are salting the leaves, blanch them first by swirling them in boling water for 10 seconds before plunging them in ice cold water. Place each leaf in the container and layer up with a sprinkle of salt, forming a lasagne of leaves and salt. Follow the instructions as for the flowers, but be aware that leaves are more fragile when they dry. Gently layer them on top of each other in an airtight container until needed. You can use *sakura* as a salty seasoning or in sweet dishes and tea – just soak them in water to remove excess saltiness before using. Use within 12 months, just as the next season of blossoms opens.

MAKES
1 × 300 ML
(10 FL OZ/1¼
CUPS)
BOTTLE OF
VINEGAR
/ PICKLE
SERVES 6

Cherry Blossom Quick-Pickled Cucumbers

Japanese cherry blossom vinegars are made by infusing freshly gathered blossoms into rice wine vinegar. This recipe will reward you with a vinegar that can turn into almost anything, from a drink with the addition of carbonated water, to a dressing for sushi, a drizzle for ice creams, or this dish – the most delicious pickle.

FOR THE VINEGAR

1 cup of cherry blossoms
300 ml (10 fl oz/1¼ cups) rice wine vinegar
sugar or honey, to sweeten

FOR THE PICKLE

3 tbsp Cherry Blossom Vinegar (see above)
1 shallot, finely diced
handful of basil and mint (or shiso leaves if you're lucky enough to have access to them), finely chopped into grass-like slivers
2 Sichuan peppercorns, crushed
pinch of salt
6 radishes, thinly sliced
1 cucumber, thinly sliced
cherry blossoms, to serve

For the vinegar, wash and dry the blossoms, ensuring any insects have crawled away. Pack the blossoms into a sterilised jar and pour over the rice vinegar. Use a clean fermentation stone or a bag filled with water to keep the blossoms under the vinegar. Seal and keep in a cupboard. After a few days, remove the stone or bag and taste the vinegar. Slowly stir in enough sugar or honey until the vinegar becomes slightly sweet but not cloyingly so – make sure the sugar is dissolved thoroughly before testing. If the flowers have sunk to the bottom of the jar, simply replace the lid, otherwise place the weight back in. After a few days, the vinegar will turn pink and take on the flavour of the blossoms. Strain the blossoms from the vinegar, pressing the flowers to extract as much flavour as possible into the vinegar.

Make the pickle by mixing together the vinegar with the shallot, most of the basil and mint (reserve a few slices for garnish), crushed peppercorns and salt. Pour over the finely sliced radishes and cucumber, and leave for a couple of hours before serving to allow the flavours to mature.

Before serving, sprinkle with cherry blossoms and the reserved slices of mint and basil.

SERVES 4

Sakura Gohan – Cherry Blossom Rice

Sakura gohan is at its most simple, salted cherry blossoms (*sakura*) with steamed rice (*gohan*) – a savoury dish that is far more than the sum of its parts. Its simplicity showcases the incredible almond flavour that salting cherry blossoms and leaves produces.

Although this recipe simple in ingredients, its success lies in how you prepare the steamed rice – the aim is to achieve a fluffy consistency rather than the sticky dense rice of sushi. A rice paddle is your ally here and will help you stir at the crucial moments without breaking the tender grains into a mush. If you want to add more flavour to your dish, adding a cup of dashi to the cooking water, a splash of sake, a piece of kombu (kelp) or a finely chopped umeboshi plum won't lessen its appeal in any way.

- 350 g (12 oz/generous 1½ cups) sushi rice
- 350 g (12 oz/1½ cups) water
- 1 tbsp *Sakura* (salted cherry blossoms, see page 63)

Firstly, steam your rice. Place the rice in a sieve and run a gentle flow of water through to get rid of any surface dust. Place the rice in a bowl of water and again gently swirl the rice until the water turns cloudy. Drain and repeat until the water remains clear. Leave the rice to sit in the last batch of water for 30 minutes.

Drain the rice and add to a pan with the measured fresh water. Bring to the boil and cook for 2 minutes before covering with a tight-fitting lid and turning down the heat to a simmer. Cook for 3 minutes, then reduce the heat right down to the lowest possible for another 5 minutes. Turn off the heat and leave to steam for another 15 minutes.

Remove the cherry blossoms from their jar, shaking any excess salt back into the jar. Chop the blossoms up finely (keep back 4 blossoms for garnish).

When the rice has finished steaming, sprinkle the chopped blossoms into the pan and carefully use your rice paddle or the edge of a spoon to cut through the rice to fluff it up and distribute the salty blossoms though the dish.

Serve in rice bowls as a springtime side dish you'll want to eat all year round.

MAKES
12 SLICES

Cherry Blossom and Leaf Milk Cake

Cherry leaves and blossoms infused in batters turn a plain cake into a light, almond-laced sponge without the expense of almonds. Milk cakes hail from equally frugal baking practices during the American Depression, when milk replaced some of the more expensive butter in cakes in an attempt to save money. Fortunately, thrift pays off and the addition of milk and cherry blossom makes a cake that is worth eating at the most decadent of high teas.

- 200 ml (7 fl oz/scant 1 cup) milk
- 240 g (8½ oz/generous 1 cup) unrefined sugar
- 4 cherry leaves
- 125 g (4½ oz) salted butter
- 4 medium eggs
- 240 g (8½ oz/scant 2 cups) self-raising flour
- 2 cups of cherry blossom petals
- 100 g (3½ oz/generous ¾ cup) icing (confectioners') sugar
- 2 tbsp lemon or cherry juice (or cherry liqueur if you have some)

Preheat the oven to 180°C (350°F/gas 4). Grease and line a 20 cm (8 in) cake tin (pan).

Gently heat the milk in a pan until warm, then remove from the heat and add 1 tablespoon of the sugar and the cherry leaves. Leave to infuse for a couple of hours.

Cream the butter and remaining sugar together, then add the eggs and flour in stages, beating until you have a thick, smooth mixture. Slowly beat in the infused milk (remove the cherry leaves) and stir until you have a smooth, velvety batter. Add 1 cup of the cherry blossom petals and fold through.

Pour the batter into the prepared tin and bake for 25 minutes, or until cooked through. Remove from the oven and leave to cool slightly before removing the cake from the tin.

When the cake is fully cooled, mix the icing sugar with the juice or liqueur and pour over the cake. The icing should be thin enough to spread out by itself, but thick enough to leave a definite covering over the cake. Scatter liberally with the remaining cherry blossoms, completely covering all the icing.

Place a piece of greaseproof paper gently on the top of the cake and lightly rub the palm of your hand over the paper, helping the blossoms to flatten to the cake. (Note: If you don't have enough blossoms to cover the cake, omit this step or the icing will stick to the paper and peel away.)

Milk cakes are best served as fresh as possible. What isn't eaten at tea time will make a beautiful dessert with cooled custard or cream.

MAKES AROUND 16–18

Sakura Mochi with Cherry Blossom Vinegar

Mochi are Japanese sweet rice snacks made from *mochigome*, a pounded glutinous rice (if you can't get hold of this rice, sushi rice will work as well). Mochi are as much an icon of Japanese food as its festivals – and mochi are eaten at many of them, including Hinamatsuri – a girls' day festival, held every March for over 900 years, where pink mochi, filled with a sweet red bean paste known as *koshian* are served with salty cherry blossom leaves and flowers.

- 500 g (1 lb 2 oz) glutinous rice (or sushi rice)
- 125 g (4½ oz/generous ½ cup) caster (superfine) sugar
- 1 tsp beetroot juice or a couple of drops of red food colouring
- 1 tsp Cherry Blossom Vinegar (page 64)
- 200 g (7 oz) *koshian* (sweet bean paste)
- 16–18 *sakura* (salted cherry leaves, see page 63)

Prior to cooking the rice, rinse it until the water runs clear, then leave it to soak in water for 30 minutes before draining.

Add the rice, 800 ml (27 fl oz/3¼ cups) fresh water and the sugar to a saucepan and bring to the boil. Simmer vigorously for 10 minutes, stirring frequently to stop the rice from sticking to the base of the pan, then remove from the heat, cover and leave to steam for 30 minutes.

Stir in the beetroot juice or food colouring and the cherry blossom vinegar before pounding the rice with a wooden spoon until it becomes sticky and pliable. With wet hands, scoop up a walnut-sized ball of rice and press into a disc in your hand. Spoon a teaspoon of the koshian into the centre of the disc, then press into a ball enclosing the filling before wrapping in a salty cherry leaf. Repeat to make the other balls. Chill in the refrigerator for a few hours to allow the aroma of the leaves to permeate into the rice. Serve within a couple of days, peeling away the cherry leaves before you eat the sticky, sweet rice.

FLAVOUR PROFILE   Perfumed · Floral · Bitter · Olive

Lilac

COMMONLY USED EDIBLE SPECIES

Syringa vulgaris (common lilac).

WHERE THEY GROW

Lilacs thrive in well-draining, fertile soils rich in organic matter. They also prefer to grow in slightly alkaline soils.

WHEN TO GATHER

Flowers — mid to late spring

You may know the story of Hermes' goat-like son Pan, who spent his days chasing the nymphs of the Arcadian forest. Syrinx was one of those he set his unwanted sights on. In her attempts to flee from his advances she ran into a river and turned herself into a reed, which Pan then pulled up to make his famous pipe. Poor Syrinx. If she had fallen into a lilac shrub, her ending might have been more fragrant but she still could have ended up as a pipe, because lilac's Latin name, *syringa*, came about because like Syrinx, the shrub can be turned into pipes. It has perfect hollow, woody stems to use to whittle flutes and pipes for minor gods or mortals.

PARTS USED

① Flowers (plus leaves and bark are used in traditional herbal medicine)

CAUTION

Avoid consuming lilac if pregnant.

For the few weeks that lilac blooms, you can eat its fresh flowers sprinkled onto cakes, drinks and salads. Although its perfume is sweet, lilac flowers taste slightly bitter, almost olive flavoured. Olives and lilacs happen to be botanical siblings, both part of the *Oleaceae* family, and when paired they bring out the best in each other. Try infusing dried lilac flowers into olive oil, or stuffing a standard olive with a few lilac petals – truly food for the gods and their long-suffering nymphs.

Capturing the sweet perfume of the flower isn't as straightforward as just eating them – their perfume is made from volatile and elusive oils, which evade capture as much as the Greek nymphs did. Fortunately, some scent can be caught by turning them into syrups, vinegars and alcohol, but the best way to harness the perfume of lilac is through a technique called *enfleurage* (the French perfumiers' trick of capturing scents), requiring nimble fingers, patience and fat. Fill a lidded container with a layer of melted fat (this has to be the kind of fat that turns solid at room temperature – traditionally animal fat, but you can use any neutral fat: coconut, shea, or palm fat will do). When your fat has turned solid, collect a freshly opened lilac head and pull off each individual flower from the head, placing each tiny bloom face down onto the fat, pressing enough so that they are in complete contact with it. Once all the flowers are on the fat, cover them with a layer of parchment or cling film (plastic wrap), making sure to squeeze out any air bubbles. Cover the container with its lid and leave at room temperature overnight. The next day, remove the flowers and replace them with another batch of fresh flowers. Repeat this process for at least 5 days. If you have the patience, you can carry on doing this for a few weeks until no more lilac flowers bloom. The more you do this, the more fragrance of the flowers will be captured in your fat.

When you've had enough of placing flowers on fat and taking them off again, you might not be convinced that there's much scent in the fat, but don't panic, there will be. Rub a little onto warm skin and the perfume will come alive. You have made a solid (edible) perfume, which can be turned into a liquid by covering with 100%-proof alcohol and macerating for a few months. The fat will release its new scent into the alcohol, giving you a hard-won lilac extract to splash into macarons, ice creams, possets and drinks at any time of the year.

If all of this sounds like far too much effort, but you still want to capture the essence of lilac, you can put enfleurage's technique to work on butter for a couple of days or even chocolate by placing a bar of chocolate in a sealed tub with lilac blooms for a day or so. (Anyone who has ever eaten a bar of chocolate that had been stored next to strong flavours can attest to chocolate's incredible ability to absorb perfume.) Perhaps if Pan had offered Syrinx lilac-flavoured truffles he would've had a better chance of holding her hand rather than a pipe.

SERVES 6

Lilac, Olive and Potato Salad

The addition of lilacs and their botanical sibling olives elevates this humble, earthy potato salad into a dish fit for the gods. It is delicious served with oily fish and green beans.

1 kg (2 lb 4 oz) new salad potatoes (waxy potatoes like Jersey or Charlottes are ideal)
100 g (3½ oz) pitted black olives
2 tbsp capers, rinsed and finely chopped
6 spring onions (scallions), finely sliced
1 small bunch of parsley, leaves and stems, finely chopped
1 small bunch of mint, leaves and stems, finely chopped
1 bunch of chives and chive flowers (wild garlic stems and flowers are great swaps if you have them), stems chopped
zest of ½ lemon
3 tbsp extra virgin olive oil
2 tbsp lilac-infused white wine vinegar (you can just use white wine vinegar if you have not made the infused version, see below)
2 lilac flower heads
salt and black pepper

TO MAKE THE LILAC-INFUSED WHITE WINE VINEGAR

200 ml (7 fl oz/scant 1 cup) white wine vinegar
2 lilac flower heads

Pull the flowers from the stem of 2 lilac flowers, and pack them into a glass jar. Pour over the white wine vinegar, cover and leave to infuse for 4–5 days before straining and bottling to use in dressings or cooking.

Scrub the potatoes and place in a pan of cold, salted water. Bring to a simmer, then cook until the potatoes become soft enough to push a fork into, but are not falling apart. Drain and leave to cool in a serving bowl.

Halve the olives and place them in a separate bowl with the capers, spring onions, parsley, mint, chive stems and lemon zest.

Pour the olive oil and infused vinegar into a jam jar with a lid, add a pinch of salt and pepper and shake until emulsified. Pour the dressing over the olive and herb mixture, stirring well so that all the ingredients are coated in oil.

When you're ready to serve, spoon the dressing mixture over the potatoes and sprinkle with torn lilac and chive flowers.

SERVES 2

Lilac Gin Sour

Lilac flower syrup is lovely drizzled onto pancakes, poached rhubarb or ice cream, but perhaps its favourite way of being consumed is in a gin sour – use a lighter gin that's not too juniper heavy to allow the flowers to showcase their flavour. Most sours use egg whites to provide the ubiquitous foam, however, apple pectin gives not only the viscosity and foam you'd associate with a sour, but also a flavour that shows off blousy lilacs to their best. If you wanted to refrain from adding alcohol, swap it for a few smashed pine shoots or blackcurrant leaves added to the cocktail shaker.

FOR THE SYRUP

- 5 lilac flower heads, freshly picked (discard any browning petals)
- 200 g (7 oz/scant 1 cup) white sugar
- 200 ml (7 fl oz/scant 1 cup) water

FOR THE COCKTAIL

- ice
- 60 ml (2 fl oz/¼ cup) Lilac Syrup (see above)
- 60 ml (2 fl oz/¼ cup) fresh lemon juice
- 120 ml gin
- 100 ml (3½ fl oz/scant ½ cup) Apple Pectin (see recipe on page 128)

To make the lilac syrup, rinse the lilac flowers to remove any bugs and dirt (lilac's scent is in the petals not the pollen, so it won't get washed away). Pull the flowers from the stems and place in a large jar.

Heat the sugar and water in a pan until the sugar dissolves and the syrup becomes clear. Leave to cool so that the syrup is hot, not boiling, then pour over the lilacs, pushing the petals down into the jar to make sure they are submerged in the syrup. (Cover the top of the syrup with a piece of parchment paper or waxed jam disc if the flowers keep rising to the top.) Cover and leave to infuse overnight.

The next day, strain the syrup through a fine sieve and pour into a bottle. It will keep in the refrigerator for a few weeks.

To make the cocktail, fill a cocktail shaker with ice and let the shaker chill for a few minutes before tipping the ice into a bowl. Pour the syrup, lemon juice, gin and apple pectin into the shaker and shake until the mixture becomes foamy. Add the ice back into the shaker (leave any melt water in the bowl) and shake again until the cocktail is well chilled.

Strain into two chilled cocktail glasses and serve.

MAKES
1 X 500 ML
(17 FL OZ/
GENEROUS
2 CUPS)
BOTTLE

Lilac Olive Oil

The scent of fresh lilacs feels very distant to the taste of olives, but smell a jar of dried lilac flowers and you'll notice an unmistakable olive oil aroma. Dried lilacs infused in olive oil don't make the oil taste perfumed, rather they make it taste like a better version of itself. They can turn a mediocre oil into one that tastes fresh, floral and fruity – olive oil that tastes of olives (but actually it's lilac).

4 lilac flower heads
500 ml (17 fl oz/2 cups) extra virgin olive oil

Place the freshly collected flower heads in a dehydrator or over a low heat source (a radiator for example) and dry the flowers thoroughly.

Pull the flowers from the dried flower head and pack into in a heatproof bottle. Pour over the olive oil and place the bottle in a pan of warm water. Set the pan over a very low heat so it just stays warm rather than simmers and heat for a couple of hours. Remove the pan from the heat and cool.

Use to make the best-dressed of salads.

MAKES 20

Lilac Chocolate Truffles

Lilac's almost bitter perfume makes a great flavour pairing with chocolate, the flecks of powdered lilac add both flavour and colour to the dark chocolate. To make sure your lilac retains its colour when you dry it, collect just-opened flowers on a dry day, discarding any that have turned brown, and dehydrate as soon as possible. If you have a dehydrator, set it at 45°C (110°F), otherwise, place your flowers on a folded up cloth on a cooling rack sat on a warm radiator. Once your flowers have completely dried, remove them from the stems and store them in an airtight jar out of direct sunlight – they can be kept for 12 months, but might lose their colour over time.

- 300 ml (10 fl oz/1¼ cups) double (heavy) cream
- 70 g (2½ oz/⅓ cup) Lilac Sugar (see page 81)
- 300 g (10½ oz) dark chocolate (80% cocoa solids), finely chopped
- 4 dried lilac flower heads

Line a 15 cm square (6 in square) tupperware container with greaseproof paper.

Place a heatproof bowl on top of a saucepan half-filled with water (ensure the base of the bowl does not touch the water) and set over a medium heat. Pour the cream and lilac sugar into the bowl and heat gently until the sugar has dissolved. Add the chopped chocolate to the cream and stir until the chocolate has dissolved. Pour the mixture into your prepared container, then place in the refrigerator to firm up.

Meanwhile, pull the dried flowers from the lilac flower heads and grind them in a coffee or spice grinder to a purple powder. Pour onto a saucer.

When the truffle mixture has set, turn it out onto a clean work surface. With a hot knife (dip the blade into boiled water), cut the slab into small squares (these truffles are very rich so err on the small side). Coat each square in the powdered lilac and chill until ready to serve.

These truffles will keep for up to a week in the refrigerator, but make sure to keep them in a very well-sealed container or they will absorb other flavours in the refrigerator.

Lilac Possets

Dainty lemon possets with crumbly biscuits are an easy, make-ahead dessert that captures the freshness of lilac flowers, their petals balancing the sweetest of puddings with delicious, ever so slightly bitter bursts of floral flavour.

MAKES 6

150 g (5½ oz/scant ¾ cup) caster (superfine) sugar
600 ml (20 fl oz/2½ cups) double (heavy) cream
3 lilac flower heads
zest and juice of 2 lemons
6 light biscuits, to serve (vanilla butter biscuits are ideal)

Place the sugar, cream and the petals from one of the lilac flowers in a heavy-based pan and heat to a simmer. Without letting the mixture boil, keep simmering for 5 minutes until the cream slightly thickens. Remove from the heat and strain the mixture through a sieve to remove the petals, then whisk in the lemon zest and juice.

Let the mixture cool slightly before stirring in most of the petals from the second lilac flower head. Pour into 6 glasses or teacups and chill for at least 3 hours before serving.

Serve scattered with a few fresh petals from the third lilac flower head, with a buttery biscuit on the side.

Lilac Sugar

Making floral sugars is as simple as infusing scented flowers in sugar. They are a great way to preserve flowers because by drying the sugar you remove risks of it going mouldy. You can even turn the sugar into a syrup, as and when you might need it; simply dissolve a spoonful of the sugar with a spoonful of warm water and a squeeze of lemon juice.

MAKES ABOUT 300 G (10½ OZ/1⅓ CUPS)

3 lilac flower heads, washed and slightly damp
300 g (10½ oz/1⅓ cups) granulated sugar

Pull the flowers away from the stalks and place them in a thin layer on the base of a flat, shallow bowl. Pour the sugar over the flowers, making sure all the flowers are submerged. Cover the bowl with a lid and place somewhere warm for 12 hours.

Remove the lid and spoon the sugar and flowers onto a flat tray. Place on a radiator or in a very low oven (50°C/120°F) to dry out. Once the sugar has dried, spoon the mixture into a food processor and blend the flowers and sugar together.

Jar and store in a cupboard. This sugar can be used in place of syrup and will keep for 6 months.

FLAVOUR PROFILE

Hosta has similar flavours to asparagus, with a slightly more nutty flavour.
The flowers have a flavour similar to artichoke hearts and broad beans, with a slight bitterness.

Hosta

COMMONLY USED EDIBLE SPECIES

Hosta montana (large-leaved hosta), *Hosta sieboldii* (small-leaved plantain lily), *Hosta crispula* (curled plantain lily), *Hosta longipes* (plantain lily), *Hosta* 'Undulata', *Hosta fortunei*.

WHERE THEY GROW

Hosta grows in a wide range of environments – according to species, they can be planted in shade, damp soil or full sun in rocky ground.

WHEN TO GATHER

Spring and early summer

All of our food and garden plants have their roots in the wild. Since we first started farming, people have propagated bigger, brighter, longer-flowering plants and sweeter vegetables bred from their wild origins into what we tend to in our gardens and cook in our kitchens today. Some plants create new varieties on their own, adapting to the terrains and locations they grow in. Hostas are amongst this group – their hybridising skills have created hundreds of variants of the sculptural, ribbed-leaved plants, ranging from lime green with stripes to almost grey blue, with heart-shaped leaves, all evolved to suit an equally wide range of environments: rocky ground, marshy soil, shade, and full sun.

PARTS USED

① Shoots
② Leaves
③ Leaf Stems
④ Flowers.

CAUTION

Hosta is toxic to cats and dogs if ingested. Do not feed them with any scraps or leftovers.

Gardeners often associate hostas with being shade-loving (and slug-beloved) plants, but take a leaf out of hosta's own gardening book and you might find that your own plant would thrive better in a sunnier, drier part of your garden than you thought. When hostas get a chance to thrive, they bulk out, creating mounds of foliage that emerge in the spring curled up like spears pushing out of the ground. And from the moment the first hosta shoots break through the warming spring soil until the last mauve flowering stem bursts open, you can harvest and eat the plant.

The new spring shoots are prized for their squeaky, crunchy stems and mild flavours, which according to the variety taste like anything from asparagus to a mild onion. In Japan and Korea, wild edibles have their own denomination of *sansai* (*san-namul* in Korea) – 'mountain vegetables'. Hostas are part of this rather elite group. Wild vegetables are often rich in vitamins and minerals, and hosta is no different.

An abundant source of easy-to-eat spring nutrition with a mild flavour that even the least adventurous children and adults love eating thinly sliced, along with carrots, cucumber and a pot of mayonnaise (if you have offspring with more adventurous tastes, you can swirl a spoon of miso into the mayo and they'll be officially eating *sansai* like the cool Japanese children do).

Hostas may have been traditionally harvested from the wild, but you can now find them when foraging in Japanese supermarkets, sold in spring, labelled with the name of *urui*. They look paler than wild hostas, as cultivated spears are grown in huge forcing sheds like rhubarb and chicory (grown in the dark to make them as tender and mild as possible – satisfying the pickiest of modern taste buds). Whether gathered from the wild or cultivated in the dark, hosta shoots are delicious paired with fish, fatty meats, nuts and salty flavours. If you have a well-established clump of hosta, you'll find that the stems unfurl over a period of weeks. Push apart the fully opened leaves and it may reveal tender new growth emerging from the ground until late spring. After the leaves open up, they start to become tougher and will need to be cooked for longer to soften. Even when the fully opened leaves are too tough to cook with, they make excellent wraps for baking fish and vegetables.

After all the leaves have opened and you think that your harvest of *sansai* is over for the year, the plant generously grows long slender flowering stems, covered in mauve, bell-like flowers, which make salad ingredients, cocktail infusions and garnishes worth climbing back up into the wild mountains (or your back garden) to collect.

SERVES 6

Hosta and Herb Quiche

Young hosta stems are a delicious springtime vegetable that rival asparagus, and make an equally delicious quiche, laced with tender spring herbs. Hosta's beautifully patterned leaves look stunning laid on the top of the quiche.

- 110 g (3¾ oz) butter
- 120 g (4 oz/1 cup) plain (all-purpose) flour
- 60 g (2 oz/generous ⅓ cup) wholewheat flour
- ½ tsp salt
- 1–2 tbsp ice-cold water
- 120 ml (4 fl oz/½ cup) double (heavy) cream
- 120 ml (4 fl oz/½ cup) milk
- 3 eggs
- ½ cup grated cheese (Gruyère, hard goat's cheese or Cheddar)
- ½ cup finely chopped dill, tarragon and mint
- 400 g (14 oz) hosta leaves and stems, stems chopped into small pieces
- salt and black pepper, to taste

Before starting to make the pastry, place your butter in the freezer for 30 minutes, or until very hard.

Sift the flours and salt into a mixing bowl and grate the butter into the flour. Rub the butter into the flour until light and crumbly. Add a spoonful of ice-cold water at a time and gently incorporate the water into the mixture. As soon as it holds together as a dough, stop working it. Press the dough into a circular disc, wrap and chill in the refrigerator for 30 minutes.

Roll out the pastry to around 5 mm (¼ in) thick and use to line a tart pan or dish. Refrigerate for at least another 30 minutes.

Meanwhile, preheat the oven to 190°C (375°F/gas 5).

Cover the pastry with a sheet of baking parchment, and add a layer of dried beans. Bake for 10 minutes before removing the beans and paper and returning to the oven for another 5–10 minutes to dry out the base. Remove from the oven and set aside.

Whisk the cream, milk and eggs together before adding the grated cheese, herbs and chopped hosta stems. Season with salt and pepper. Pour the mixture into the pastry case, then lay the hosta leaves on top.

Bake for 25–30 minutes until the quiche is golden but still slightly wobbly. Remove from the oven and let cool for a few minutes before serving.

SERVES 4 AS A SIDE SALAD

Hosta Flower, Artichoke, Asparagus and Broad Bean Salad

Bite into a hosta flower and you may pick up a hint of its family member asparagus, but you might also taste broad (fava) bean or artichoke. It's almost as if evolution had read a cookbook on Italian summer salads – especially since hosta flowers open just as artichokes swell, broad beans plump and asparagus is still (only just) in season. If you don't have access to fresh artichoke or broad beans, tinned artichoke hearts and frozen, shelled broad beans will work well and save you hours of podding and peeling.

- 100 g (3½ oz/scant 1 cup) shelled broad (fava) beans
- 200 g (7 oz) tinned or fresh artichoke hearts, drained and rinsed, cut into bite-size pieces
- 100 g (3½ oz/scant 1 cup) rocket (arugula)
- 20 g (¾ oz/2 tbsp) toasted pine nuts
- 1 shallot, finely sliced
- 30 g (1 oz) Parmesan, shaved
- a few spears of raw asparagus
- 6 hosta flowers (approx. 15 g/½ oz), to serve

FOR THE DRESSING

- 50 ml (1¾ fl oz/3½ tbsp) olive oil
- 25 ml (1½ tbsp) lemon juice
- 1 good pinch of salt

Boil the beans in a pan of water for a couple of minutes until tender, then drain and refresh under cold running water to stop them from cooking. Place the beans in a bowl with the artichoke hearts, rocket, pine nuts, shallot and Parmesan, then shave over strips of asparagus.

For the dressing, shake the olive oil, lemon juice and salt together in a jar, then pour over the salad. Pull the hosta flowers from their main stems and scatter over the salad just before serving. Serve with a savoury tart or breads (Italian, of course).

Hosta Wrapped in Bacon

Hosta shoots, like asparagus, have a flavour that cuts through the fat and salt of bacon. Wrapping hosta shoots in the cured meat is a popular culinary pastime of hosta eaters. If you like even fattier meats, you can use pancetta or lardo in place of the bacon.

SERVES 4

olive oil, for greasing
12 hosta shoots
6 slices of bacon (12 if your shoots are very large)
salt and black pepper, to taste

Preheat the oven to 180°C (350°F/gas 4). Lightly grease a baking sheet with olive oil.

Wash the hosta shoots, making sure no soil is caught in the furled shoots.

Cut the slices of bacon in half (leave them whole if your hosta shoots are very large), then wrap each shoot in a slice of bacon and place on the prepared baking sheet. Season with salt and pepper.

Bake in the oven for 15 minutes, or until the hosta has started to soften and the bacon is crisp.

Hosta with Walnuts and Miso

Young hosta stems are often grown like chicory and rhubarb in forcing sheds, producing a tender, almost white stem – these are known as snow leaves or icicles in Japan. You can force your own hosta by placing a bucket or pot over a clump of emerging hostas. The forced shoots are tender enough to serve raw and are often accompanied with a miso sauce. This *kurumi miso* sauce includes walnuts, which showcases the slightly nutty flavour hostas hide in their stems.

SERVE 4 AS A SIDE DISH

4 tbsp red miso
1½ tbsp sugar
2 tbsp sake
1 tbsp water, or as needed
30 g (1 oz/¼ cup) walnuts, dry-roasted in a pan and ground into a coarse paste
20 young hosta stems

Heat the miso, sugar and sake together in a pan for 2 minutes, stirring all the time to prevent the sauce from burning. Add water if the sauce looks too dry – it should become glossy and thick but still pourable. Remove the pan from the heat and stir in the walnut paste, again adding a little water if the sauce is too thick.

Slice the hosta stems into 5 cm (2 in) pieces and place in a pan of boiling water to blanch for 30 seconds before plunging into cold water. If your hosta has a tough skin, gently peel it away like you would rhubarb before serving at room temperature with a spoonful of the miso sauce. This recipe is delicious served as a snack or with rice and slow-cooked pork.

MAKES 2 LITRES (68 FL OZ/ 8½ CUPS)

Hosta Flower and Melon Punch

Hosta flowers bloom at the height of summer and their flowers are not only beautiful in garden borders, but also in salads and drinks – especially in summer punches, enjoyed on long, balmy evenings with groups of friends. Drinks like punches made in jugs mean that you can spend less time mixing individual servings, but do mean that you might be serving a drink that's not sweet or bitter enough for your friends' individual tastes. Hosta flowers aren't overly sweet, and like the flowers, this punch is neither very sweet or bitter, so add a teaspoon of honey if you have a sweet tooth, or a splash of melon rind bitters if you're that way inclined.

- 2 cantaloupe melons
- 250 ml (8½ fl oz/1 cup) vodka, plus 100ml (3½ fl oz/scant ½ cup) to make melon bitters
- 1 dash of melon bitters
- 1 cup of hosta flowers, plus extra to serve
- 25 g (1 oz/2 tbsp) granulated sugar
- handful of mint, plus extra to serve
- 1 bottle of dry white wine (chenin blanc or sauvignon blanc)
- 1 litre (34 fl oz/4¼ cups) club soda or sparkling water, to top up
- honey, to serve (optional)

To make the melon rind bitters, wash and chop the rind of ¼ melon and place in a blender with 100 ml (3½ fl oz/scant ½ cup) vodka. Purée until smooth, then strain through a fine sieve into a bottle. (A bottle with a dropper or pipette would be ideal.)

A few hours before you serve the drink, scoop out large balls of flesh from the first melon. If you don't have a melon baller, cube the melon into ice-cube sizes. Place on a freezer-proof tray and freeze. At the same time, pull the hosta flowers from the stems and place in a pestle and mortar along with the sugar. Smash the flowers into the sugar (they'll turn it pale purple), then pour over the remaining 250 ml (3½ fl oz/scant ½ cup) vodka, decant into a jar and let sit for a few hours.

Purée the flesh of the second melon, then strain the juice into a bowl through a sieve (you can use the leftover pulp in sorbets).

When you are almost ready to serve, place the mint in a jug, followed by some of the frozen melon balls/cubes. Pour over the melon juice, white wine and infused vodka, then stir and chill before serving.

To serve, place the remaining frozen melon balls/cubes into tumblers, pour over the punch and top with club soda. Add a drop of melon rind bitters or a spoonful of honey to each drink, stir and garnish with hosta flowers and mint leaves.

FLAVOUR PROFILE Sweet · Nectar-like · Pea

Wisteria

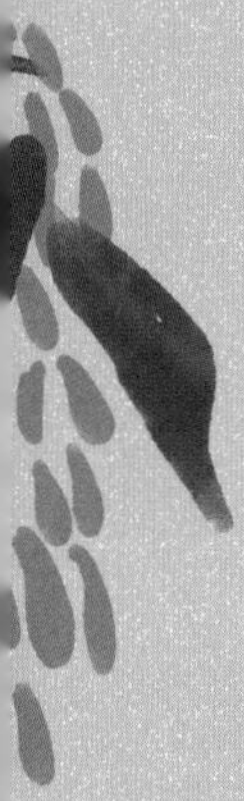

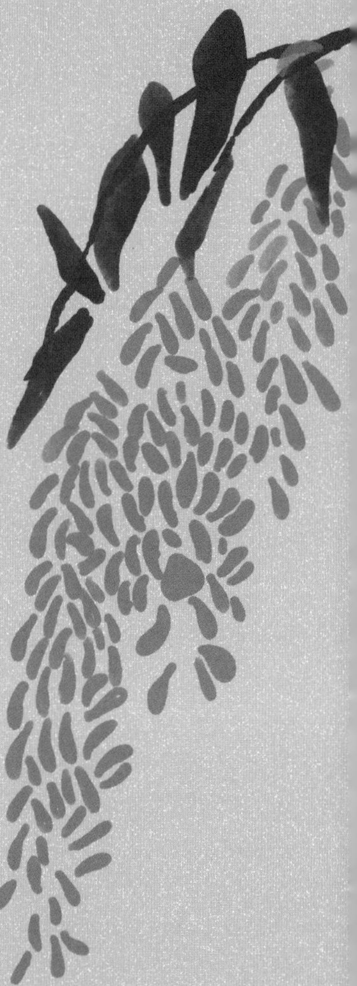

COMMONLY USED EDIBLE SPECIES

Wisteria sinensis (Chinese wisteria), *Wisteria floribunda* (Japanese wisteria).

WHERE THEY GROW

Full sun or partial shade in neutral or slightly acidic soil.

WHEN TO GATHER

Mid–late spring, when the flowers are just opening.

In 1894, Alice Brugman from Sierra Madre in California spent 75 cents on a little Chinese wisteria. She planted it, like most do, against her wall; probably hoping it would cover the façade with blossoms in spring. The plant in fact grew way beyond that wall – like a triffid it enveloped the entire house, eventually collapsing the home that it was planted to adorn. The same wisteria is now visited each spring by huge crowds who stand where the old house once did, under a roof of fragrant flowers supported by a vast network of scaffolding, because the 75-cent wisteria that Alice bought is now the largest flowering plant alive – one of the seven horticultural wonders of the world.

PARTS USED

① Flowers

CAUTION

Do not confuse wisteria flowers for lethally poisonous laburnum. Only use the flowers as all other parts of the plant are toxic – including the flower stems, leaves and seeds (see opposite for more information on how to prepare the flowers).

It's not just in Sierra Madre that buildings are engulfed by wisteria. Each spring, millions of houses across the world disappear behind its blooms – fortunately, unlike Alice's wisteria, it simply decorates rather than destroys homes. If you do happen to have what appears to be a triffid-like version, move it into your garden to grow up a frame and you'll create a springtime cathedral of mauve to sit under and admire its heavenly scent. Across Japan, parks are filled with wisterias growing just like this, supported by scaffolds, which create covered walkways of flowers. And, as is the style in Japan, people come in their droves to admire the flowers. Take a look at photos taken in Ashikaga Park in Toyko and you'll see people standing under these purple caves of flowers, often holding ice creams and *wagashi* sweets that match the hue of the flowers. Their ice creams and sweets may look like wisteria, but they're style over substance as they're dyed with food colouring and artificial flavourings rather than made with the flower itself. This is a shame, because wisteria eating is without a doubt just as satisfying as wisteria gazing.

Wisteria flowers taste utterly ambrosial – with a sweet, pea-like flavour that's fit for both gods and angelic beings to graze on as they sit in the heavens, strumming their harps (or whatever they do up there). The nod to peas in their flavour is more than a coincidence, because they're both part of the *Fabaceae* family of plants – home to everything from tiny wild vetches to vast acacia trees. Look at individual wisteria flowers and you'll recognise the shape of the blooms from the vegetables you might grow in your gardens. Older wisteria flowers will even have tiny, thin fruits forming inside, which will eventually grow into long pods. But, unlike peas, these seeds and pods are inedible, since wisteria contains a toxic compound that renders all parts other than the mauve flowers poisonous (some cultures have mastered ways to remove the toxin, but that's for another book – we're sticking to the flowers).

Before you get scared by toxins in a cookery book, take a moment to consider the other plants we eat in the pea family – they often come with a side helping of compounds that need extracting to make them safe. Have you ever eaten a raw or dried kidney bean? Hopefully not, because it would make you very ill indeed – soaking and cooking these beans not only makes them easy to eat, but stops them being very poisonous.

Whilst many people are happy to eat the flowers freshly plucked from the vine, in countries where the wisteria flowers are most frequently eaten, a few simple steps are taken to ensure they are completely safe to eat. And following the lead of people who have a history of safely eating something is always a wise thing to do. Firstly, collect the flowers when they're just about to open or just after they have. If they have opened, pull out the central sepals and stamen, especially if any tiny seed pods are forming. (This might seem like a faff, but removing the bitter shells from broad/fava beans takes far longer to do – and with a glass of something delicious in hand makes for a leisurely half hour.) Soaking the flowers in water or a salty brine before you use them is an additional belt-and-braces way to break down any remaining toxin traces that could remain.

Once you have removed the inner parts of the flower, the world is your ambrosial oyster. In Turkey, where sour drinks known as sherbets quench thirsts, the flowers are soaked in water overnight before adding sugar, lemon juice and lemon salt to make *Mor Salkim Serbeti* – wisteria sherbet drink. The leftover flowers aren't wasted (especially after they've been painstakingly processed), they're turned into a wisteria jam (cooked with apple pectin, sugar and water until the liquid has thickened and the flowers become translucent – if you like the sound of wisteria jam, follow the recipe for Peony Jam on page 128, swapping the bitter peony petals for the sweet wisteria.)

If you don't have the time or inclination to pull out the inner workings of each little flower, leave aside any flowers that have tiny pea pods forming inside and turn the rest into cooked dishes like fritters, cakes and syrups. In Beijing, the homeland of Alice's giant Chinese wisteria, wisteria flower cakes (a regional version of China's famous mooncake pastries) are stuffed with jam made from the flower and eaten during the autumnal moon-gazing festival. How much more apt could a food be, to be eaten whilst you gaze into the sky at the full moon, than heavenly tasting wisteria?

MAKES 12

Wisteria, Pea and Broad Bean Bruschetta

Late spring sees the arrival of the first fresh beans and peas of the year. Why not sit in time-honoured fashion on your sun-warmed kitchen step podding a bowl of legumes? If your kitchen door is surrounded by wisteria, you're in romantic luck, and can pluck yourself a few flowers to make this canapé of spring. (If you haven't a step or a wisteria, go and ask someone very nicely for a few flowers; they might even let you pod your beans at their kitchen door if you're lucky.) Served on bruschetta-style bread, these make beautiful canapés, starters or the most elegant sandwich ever eaten on a doorstep.

- 200 g (7 oz) broad (fava) beans
- 200 g (7 oz) fresh peas (or frozen petit pois)
- 1 garlic clove, peeled
- 1 tbsp chopped fresh mint
- 2 handfuls of mixed baby salad leaves or pea shoots
- flowers pulled from 2 wisteria flower heads (sepals and pistils removed)
- 2 tbsp white wine vinegar
- 4 tbsp extra virgin olive oil
- 2 tbsp grape juice
- salt and black pepper, to taste
- 12 slices of toasted ciabatta or baguette, to serve

Bring a pan of water to the boil, add the beans and peas and cook for 2 minutes. Drain and immediately refresh under cold running water, then drain again. Use your fingernail to break open the shell around the broad beans and gently squeeze the beans out of their shells (these are bitter and well worth the time to remove). Shell the peas if their skins are tough, otherwise you can leave them in their skins.

Rub the peeled garlic clove vigorously around the inside of a bowl, then discard. Place half of the peas and beans into the bowl and use the back of a fork to press down on them until they are lightly smashed. Stir in the chopped mint, season with salt and pepper and set aside.

Mix the remaining peas and beans with the pea shoots and wisteria flowers. Mix together the white wine vinegar, olive oil and grape juice, and use to dress the salad.

Spoon the smashed bean and pea mixture onto toasted bruschetta, and top with the salad. The canapes are perfect to have with drinks or as a light snack.

SERVES 4

Wisteria with Griddled Lettuce, Courgettes and Mozzarella

Wisteria flowers bloom just as the first, sweet courgettes (zucchini) and crunchy lettuces grown in sunlight, rather than under glass, start appearing in gardens and greengrocers. The start of salad-eating season deserves to be celebrated with the flavours of the summer to come. Should you be making this recipe on a hot summer's day, and the thought of standing over a griddle doesn't appeal, simply use the courgettes and lettuce raw – just make sure that your courgettes are mild and fresh as the daisies that'll be blooming alongside them.

1 tbsp white wine vinegar
1 small garlic clove, crushed
3 tbsp olive oil, plus extra for cooking
½ tsp honey or Wisteria Syrup (see opposite)
6 small courgettes (zucchini)
2 little gem lettuce hearts
handful of basil leaves
1 ball of mozzarella
1 cup of individual wisteria flowers, pulled from the stem (sepals and pistils removed)
salt, to taste

Whisk together the vinegar, garlic, olive oil and honey or syrup, adding salt to taste. Set aside.

Heat a griddle or frying pan (skillet) until hot.

Slice the courgettes into 5 mm (¼ in) thick rounds and cut the little gem lettuces in half lengthways. Toss both in olive oil before placing on the hot griddle or pan. Cook for a few minutes, turning until seared on each side. Transfer to a serving bowl and leave to cool slightly before tossing with the salad dressing.

Just before serving, tear up the basil and mozzarella, and sprinkle over the salad along with the wisteria flowers. Serve with bread, salami and warm sun.

Wisteria Syrup

If any food was to be titled ambrosia of the gods, it would be nectary wisteria syrup. A perfect flavour that captures warm days of late spring in drink form. You can drizzle the syrup on sweet things, stir it into cream, over fruit or onto salads. If you are so inclined, try blending equal amounts of syrup with the smoothest vodka you can afford to make a sweet liqueur to toast the spring with.

MAKES ABOUT 350 ML (12 FL OZ/ SCANT 1½ CUPS)

350 ml (12 fl oz/scant 1½ cups) water
350 g (generous 1½ cups) granulated sugar
100 g (3½ oz) wisteria flowers (removed from the main flowering stem)

Put the water and sugar in a pan and heat until the sugar has dissolved. Turn the heat off as soon as the syrup is clear and leave to cool slightly until warm (like many floral syrups, wisteria is best infused in warm rather than hot liquid). Press the wisteria flowers into the warm syrup, cover and leave to infuse overnight.

The next day, strain and pour into sterilised bottles. The flowers will still contain delicious flavour and texture, and can be stirred into sliced strawberries, cream or even into vodka to make a small but delectable batch of wisteria liqueur. The syrup will keep for a few weeks in the refrigerator.

Wisteria, Strawberries and Cream

Wimbledon in London is not only home to the famous lawn tennis club, but also to rows of elegant town houses that are covered in well-pruned wisterias. It's almost as if the houses are proudly wearing the tennis club's colours of purple and green. If you have been to Wimbledon you'll know that eating a bowl of strawberries and cream is almost as important as the tennis itself. Next time you go, slip a tiny bottle of wisteria syrup in your pocket to drizzle over your strawberries. A scattering of a few flowers would even give you extra points for staying on brand – game, set and match to you if you do.

SERVES 4

300 ml (10 fl oz/1¼ cups) whipping cream
3 tbsp Wisteria Syrup (see left)
200 g (7 oz) strawberries, halved
flowers from 2 wisteria flower heads (with the stamens and pistils removed)

Whip the cream until soft and fluffy, then stir in the wisteria syrup. Spoon onto dessert plates and top with strawberries before scattering with the flowers. Eat on a grassy lawn, tennis racket at your side.

SERVES 4

Wisteria Beignets with Orange Blossom Crème Fraîche

Beignets are a delicious way to turn fleeting flowers into a substantial dessert. Serve drizzled with crème fraîche perfumed with honey or orange blossom.

When using wisteria the whole raceme (or flower cluster) is battered, including the inedible main stem, but only the flowers are eaten. To make sure none of your guests eat the stem, you can serve the flowers already pulled away from it, scattered over the crème fraîche.

FOR THE ORANGE BLOSSOM CRÈME FRAÎCHE

50 g (1¾ oz/scant ¼ cup) cream cheese
350 g (12 oz/1½ cups) crème fraîche
30 g (1 oz/¼ cup) icing (confectioners') sugar
1 tsp orange blossom water

FOR THE BEIGNETS

8 wisteria flower racemes
1 tbsp brandy
1 tbsp caster (superfine) sugar, plus extra for dusting
vegetable oil, for deep-frying
250 g (9 oz/2 cups) plain (all-purpose) flour
½ tsp salt
150 ml (5 fl oz/scant ⅔ cup) sparkling wine or water
200 ml (7 fl oz/scant 1 cup) milk
2 tbsp melted butter
2 egg whites

For the orange blossom crème fraîche, whisk the cream cheese in a bowl until smooth, before folding in the crème fraîche, icing sugar and orange blossom water. Refrigerate until needed (it will keep for a day in the refrigerator).

For the beignets, sprinkle the flowers with the brandy and a spoonful of sugar and leave to macerate for 30 minutes.

Heat a deep pan of vegetable oil to 175°C (325°F).

Sift the flour and salt into a bowl, then gently stir in the sparkling wine (or water), milk and melted butter. Beat the egg whites until stiff, then carefully fold them in. Dip the flowers into the batter, then carefully lower into the hot oil and deep-fry until golden. Remove the flowers with a slotted spoon and drain on paper towels before dusting with sugar.

Serve immediately with the cold crème fraîche.

To eat, pull away the flowers from the main stem and dip into the crème fraîche. Remember the stem is toxic and should not be eaten.

FLAVOUR PROFILE

FLOWERS Cool · Astringent · Fruity · Musky · Citrussy (according to variety)

ROSEHIPS Sweet · Sour, Apple · Orange · Tomato

LEAVES Tannic

Rose

COMMONLY USED EDIBLE SPECIES

All roses are edible, but only scented rose petals have the classic rose flavour.

WHERE THEY GROW

Rich, well-drained soil. Love clay and full sun, but will cope with partial shade. Feed and prune for optimal growth.

WHEN TO GATHER

Roses flower from late spring until the autumn (fall). Most varieties have their largest display of blooms in early summer. Some varieties will only flower once, but others will keep flowering (known as repeat-flowering roses). Dead head the wilted flowers to encourage new flowers.

Rosehips can be gathered from late summer until the winter, according to the species.

Of all the plants in this book, you're probably most likely to already have eaten roses, whether in a sticky piece of Turkish delight, ground into North African spice blends, sprinkled onto a cake or in a syrup or flower water splashed over fruit salads. Rose petals are one of the most widely used – and loved – of edible flowers.

PARTS USED

① Flowering buds
② Petals
③ Hips (fruit)
④ Leaves

How long we have known roses are edible is unclear, but it would be a fairly educated guess to think that our flower-eating ancestors (*hominini*) were probably drawn to the plump, sweet-smelling petals and fruity hips that grew amongst the rest of their wild plant feast. What is known with certainty is that roses date back millions of years, and by the time we took our first steps as humans, the flowers would've sweetened their way. As far back as the ancient Indus civilisation, wild roses were harvested and distilled to produce rose oils and rose water. Simultaneously, thousands of miles away in Mesopotamia, stills were likewise being filled with the scented petals to make huge amounts of the perfumed water. Two civilisations, thousands of miles apart, both extracting the oils and waters from roses in exactly the same way we do today. Perhaps both cultures used the waters they distilled to flavour food or drink, or perhaps they used them to cool fevered brows – just as the flowers are used in Ayurvedic medicine today. Whatever their motivation, rose petals like strewing herbs (sweet-smelling herbs strewn over the floor of dwellings to mask unpleasant odours), are scattered throughout the ancient historical texts of vast empires, connecting symbolism, religion, medicine and food in a way that has never been broken.

Ancient civilisations used wild-harvested roses, but today you are more likely to have access to cultivated varieties – larger roses, available in a rainbow of colours and with multiple scents. It's another ancient civilisation we have to thank for the cultivation of roses that led to the thousands of varieties we have today: China. Chinese philosopher Confucius recorded that the emperors of China were so enchanted by roses that there were hundreds of books on the plant's cultivation in the Emperor's library. The wealthy in China were so in love with the plant that roses were grown in preference to other food crops – a fixation that repeated itself in the Roman Empire, where swathes of farmland were given over to huge rose gardens.

Rose's long hold over us shows no sign of abating. As was the case in ancient China and the Roman Empire, huge amounts of roses are still grown to provide the scented water and dried rose petals you might have in your cupboard right now, from the rose city of Pushkar in Rajasthan to Bulgaria, the home of 'Rose Valley', where a vast number of farms cultivate the flower to be dried and distilled into rose water and that most precious of oils, rose otto. To obtain just 5 ml of oil requires over 20 kg (44 lb) flowers (that's a lot of roses and a very expensive oil).

If you don't have access to quite that many roses but would like to make your own rose water flavouring, fortunately a simple bowlful of fragrant petals will provide you with something delicious for the cost of heating a pan on the stove. Find a large pan and a small heatproof bowl that will fit inside with lots of room around it. Pack freshly gathered scented rose petals into the pan and cover with water. Place the bowl in the pan, then cover the pan with an inverted lid. Fill the top of the lid with ice and you have made a makeshift still. Place your still over a very gentle heat. The rose-scented water in the pan will start to evaporate. As the water hits the chilled inverted lid, the steam will condense and drip into the bowl. When about half of the water has collected in the bowl, turn off the heat and remove the bowl from the pan. Leave to cool, then taste – you will have a rose-flavoured distilled water. Pour into a sterilised bottle and use to flavour your food, or to spray on your face to cool yourself down. Revel in your fragrant connection with your rose-scented ancestors.

How to Dry Rose Petals

Drying your own fragrant roses at their peak will give you an ingredient that can be used in teas, crumbled into desserts and ground into spice mixes.

The ideal time to collect rose petals for drying is in the morning, after any dew has dried off but before the heat of the sun has had a chance to evaporate the perfumed oils. Roses are at their prime for flavour just as they have opened, but if you don't want to miss out on a floral display in your garden, gathering your petals when the flower has fully opened but just before the petals start falling will still give you beautiful flavour.

If you have a repeat-flowering rose, snip off the whole flower head (this will encourage new buds to form rather than putting energy into forming mature hips). Separate the petals from the flower head and lay them in a single layer on a piece of cloth. Place in a dehydrator or airing cupboard and leave to dry for at least 12 hours. Once all the petals have become crumbly, immediately seal them in an airtight container. If they are left out before jarring, they can rehydrate, quickly becoming soft and discoloured, which affects their flavour.)

Store in a dry cupboard away from direct sunlight for up to a year.

MAKES ENOUGH TO FILL A 100 G (3½ OZ) JAR/ SERVES 4

Rose el Hanout with a Warm Green Bean, Onion and Lemon Salad

The aromatic flavour of *ras el hanout* is synonymous with Morocco, where since ancient times spices would finish their epic journeys, having started in the furthest tips of East Asia and Africa, being distributed along the fragrant spice roads before ending up at the northern markets. Spice vendors would lure customers with tales of how to use their wares, giving tastes of their best ingredients in blends known as *ras el hanout*, or 'top of the shop'. Each trader had their own blend, sometimes showcasing up to 30 spices, flowers and herbs.

Rose el hanout is a version of the spice blend that uses a far shorter list of ingredients and a quantity of roses that would make an ancient trader wince at the expense. Fortunately, roses are far cheaper to use from your own garden. Combining your own freshly gathered and dried roses with an equal weight of spices makes this garden-plucked version of *ras el hanout* top of any shop. It's delicious sprinkled over meats, vegetables or stirred through grains such as couscous. If you have pink or red roses in your blend, you'll find their vibrant colour leeches out into oil or lemon juice, giving a pink flush as vibrant as the flavour.

This salad dish is at home with myriad other flavours – it can seamlessly infiltrate a fragrant Indian feast or a Middle Eastern platter, and is equally as delicious chilled and served alongside smoked fish and new potatoes.

FOR THE ROSE EL HANOUT

1 tsp lavender flowers
1 tsp ground cinnamon
5 cloves
1 whole star anise
½ tsp black peppercorns
1 tsp allspice berries
½ tsp cardamom seeds (released from their green pods, discarding the pods)
20 g (¾ oz) dried rose petals (dehydrated from about 140 g/4½ oz fresh rose petals)
1 tsp fennel seeds
1 tsp cumin seeds
1 tsp coriander seed

Start with the rose el hanout. Place the lavender flowers, ground cinnamon, cloves, star anise, peppercorns, allspice berries and cardamom seeds into a mixing bowl with half of the dried rose petals.

In a small dry pan, gently heat the fennel, cumin and coriander seeds, shaking the pan as the seeds warm through to prevent them from burning. When they begin to release a toasted scent and start popping, pour them straight into the mixing bowl, stirring them into the other ingredients. Transfer the mixture to a spice or coffee bean grinder and grind to the consistency of fine sand. Add the remaining dried petals to the powdery mix and blend for a few seconds to create flecks of rose petals that run through the spice blend. Spoon into in an airtight container and store in a dry, dark cupboard. It will last indefinitely but is at its most fragrant used within 6 months.

For the salad, heat 1 tablespoon of the oil in a heavy frying pan (skillet) over a medium heat. Add the beans and cook until they are softening and starting to char, tossing them from time to time so they cook evenly. Remove the beans with a slotted spoon to a plate. Add the sliced onions with the salt and remaining tablespoon of oil, and cook until golden and starting to caramelise. Add the beans back to the pan and keep the mixture warm until needed.

FOR THE SALAD

2 tbsp olive oil
250 g (9 oz) green beans, topped and tailed (or thinly sliced runner beans)
1 white onion, thinly sliced
pinch of salt
1 heaped tsp Rose el Hanout (see opposite)
juice of ½ lemon
1 tbsp hazelnut oil (or olive oil)
handful of toasted hazelnuts, roughly chopped (optional)

To make the dressing, combine the rose el hanout with the lemon juice and oil in a jar and mix together (if you have used dark roses, the dressing will turn pink).

Pile the beans and onions into a shallow dish and drizzle over the dressing before serving sprinkled with the toasted hazelnuts, if using.

SERVES 4

Rose Petal Arrabbiata Sauce

Rose petals are a key ingredient in Ayurvedic food and medicine, used to almost miraculously cool the heat of summer. The fragrant petals can help to calm the burn of chilli peppers without removing their delicious sweet, fruity flavours. The most famous rose and chilli combination is found in jars of Tunisian rose harissa, which tastes less fiery but no less flavoursome than the petal-less version of the sauce. Here, they work to calm an arrabbiata, the 'angry sauce' that hails from near the ancient rose gardens of the Roman Empire, leaving it with a more soothing taste, laced with a delicious reminder of its fiery nature.

Arrabbiata is traditionally eaten stirred through penne or spaghetti, served by itself or with burrata cheese, another taste-bud-cooling ally.

800 g (1 lb 12 oz) tinned tomatoes (plum or cherry)
70 g (2½ oz) fragrant rose petals, freshly gathered (or 10 g/½ oz dried rose petals)
1 tbsp extra virgin olive oil, plus extra to serve
10 g (½ oz) butter
1 white onion, finely chopped
6 garlic cloves, minced
1 tsp chilli (hot pepper) flakes
1 tbsp red wine vinegar or balsamic vinegar
handful of fresh basil leaves, torn (optional)
salt and black pepper, to taste
cooked pasta of choice, to serve

Place half of the tomatoes in a food processor with half of the rose petals and blitz until smooth.

Heat the olive oil and butter in a sauté pan over a medium-low heat, add the onion and sauté until it is turning a soft golden colour, around 10 minutes. Stir in the garlic and chilli flakes, and cook for 30 seconds before adding the vinegar and all of the tomatoes (including the blitzed ones), breaking up any large lumps of tomatoes with a fork. Simmer over a low heat for up to 1 hour until thick and glossy.

Finely slice the remaining rose petals into slivers about the size of a blade of grass and stir in half of them for the last few minutes of cooking. Season to taste.

Stir your freshly cooked pasta through the sauce, and serve with a drizzle of oil, strewn with the fresh basil (if using) and the remaining rose petal slivers.

MAKES A 250ML (8 FL OZ/ 1 CUP) BOTTLE

Rose Petal Preserve

Rose petal preserve sits halfway between a syrup and jam. A thick pouring syrup, unashamedly sweet, you might wince at the amount of sugar in the recipe, but rest assured you'll just need a dot of syrup to sweeten dishes. There are few things more comforting in winter than a tiny drizzle of this preserve swirled into porridge – a hint of warmer, fragrant days. It is also delicious on cheese, stirred into cream, dissolved into warm milk for the most comforting of bedtime drinks, or stir a teaspoonful into sparkling wine for a more grown-up beverage.

The base of rose petals can be bitter. As this recipe is purely about the sweet, to make the finest preserve harvest your petals by snipping them away from the flower head, leaving the bitter ends behind (you can add these to a little bottle of vodka to extract the bitterness for use in the finest floral cocktails).

250 g (9 oz) granulated sugar
100 ml (3½ fl oz) water
50 ml (1¾ fl oz) lemon juice, strained
50 ml (1¾ fl oz) orange juice, strained
100 g (3½ oz) freshly harvested and washed scented rose petals (about 6 roses)

Place the sugar and water in a pan and dissolve over a gentle heat. Keep a careful watch over the pan, stirring to avoid the sugar catching on the base (this would make the syrup taste caramelised). Once the syrup is clear, turn the heat to its lowest setting, stir in the lemon and orange juice and press in the washed rose petals. Stir continuously for around 30 minutes – you just want the syrup to be hot rather than simmering as this can affect the flavour.

Strain the hot syrup and bottle in sterilised bottles. This will keep for 6 months.

The spent rose petals can be blended with sugar and dried out to make rose petal sugar, puréed into a thick paste to use as a spread or stirred into a bottle of vodka to make a rose petal liqueur.

Sweet Rose Dukkah

MAKES A 500 ML (17 FL OZ/ GENEROUS 2 CUP) JAR

Rose petals have a long and happy history of being paired with spices and nuts. This blend of cardamom, saffron, vanilla, nuts and rose petals, makes a sugar-free sweet flavouring to sprinkle on yoghurt, cakes and strawberries. Sweetening coffee with a teaspoonful of dukkah in your cafetière will transport your 11-o'clock break to sunnier climes.

- 50 g (1¾ oz) hazelnuts
- 50 g (1¾ oz) unsalted shelled pistachios
- 50 g (1¾ oz) dried rose petals
- 1 tsp ground cardamom
- 1 vanilla pod, split and seeds scraped out
- 0.5 g (1 packet) saffron

Toast the hazelnuts in a 150°C (300°F/gas 2) oven for 10 minutes, or until starting to turn golden.

Place the toasted hazelnuts and pistachios in a food processor and pulse until they are broken into small grainy pieces. Add most of the rose petals along with the cardamon and vanilla seeds, then pulse again until the rose petals are broken down into flecks. Add the saffron strands and reserved rose petals and give the whole mixture a final pulse.

Spoon into a jar with a tight-fitting lid and store in a cool, dark cupboard for up to 3 months.

MAKES 300 ML (10 FL OZ/ 1¼ CUPS)

Rosehip and Horseradish Dipping Sauce

Rosehips are renowned for their vitamin C content – during World War II, when imported food was a rarity, children in Britain were sent out to gather rosehips, which were made into vast amounts of syrup and given to the same children in place of the imported fruit they no longer had access to. Rosehips are a powerhouse of nutrition, also containing vitamins B and E, along with important immune-boosting antioxidants and acids. Whatever their size or shape, all rosehips are edible and delicious. With a flavour somewhere between orange, tomato and apple, rosehips can turn their hands to sweet things, such as the syrup made during the rationing years, or can be used as a vibrant, tart ingredient with unlikely allies like horseradish – pungent and unapologetically savoury.

Rosehip and horseradish dipping sauce crosses the boundaries of sweet and savoury in a plate-lickingly delicious way. This drizzling condiment is absolutely lovely for coating thin slithers of raw beetroot, smoked salmon or even used as a glaze for hams. Rosehips ripen and horseradish comes into peak season just as winter starts setting in, and preparations for Christmas eating start in earnest. Rosehip and horseradish dipping sauce deserves a rightful place on the list of things to make, and to serve, on Christmas Day.

150 g (5½ oz) rosehips, washed
1 large cooking apple, washed and chopped into small pieces (including the core and skin)
about 200 ml (7 fl oz/scant 1 cup) apple cider vinegar
about 200 g (7 oz/generous 1 cup) granulated sugar
10 cm (4 in) piece of horseradish root
¼ tsp chilli (red pepper) flakes
½ tsp ground sumac (or 1 tsp sumac berries)

Place the rosehips and chopped apple in a saucepan, cover with water and simmer until the rosehips and apple have completely softened (you will need to stir the fruit to stop it from sticking to the bottom of the pan), then squash thoroughly with a potato masher. (If the mixture feels thick, add a cup of water to loosen it.) Once the fruit has broken up into a pulp, strain it through a muslin-lined sieve into a measuring jug. When all the liquid has dripped out of the sieve, pull the corners of the cloth together and squeeze out any remaining liquid (this may come out as a thicker purée – that's fine – keep squeezing until nothing else comes out of the cloth and the pulp inside is quite dry). You should have about 200 ml (7 fl oz/scant 1 cup) juice.

Pour the juice into a pan with the same amount of vinegar and sugar (one part rosehip juice, one part vinegar, one part sugar). Bring the mixture to the boil and cook until the sugar has dissolved.

Remove the pan from the heat and let it cool for a few minutes before finely grating the horseradish straight into the sauce, making sure to push it into the sauce as it falls into the pan. Stir in the chilli flakes and sumac.

Pour into sterilised bottles. Store at room temperature and the sauce will last for up to 12 months.

FLAVOUR PROFILE ROOTS Earthy · Creamy · Bitter · Astringent FLOWER Perfumed · Bitter · Chicory · Rose

Peony

COMMONLY USED EDIBLE SPECIES

Paeonia lactiflora (Chinese peony).

WHERE THEY GROW

Thrives in full sun with a rich, fertile and well-draining soil.

WHEN TO GATHER

Roots – autumn (fall) and winter (best done when you have a large clump to divide)

Flowers – midsummer

Peonies are one of the most anticipated but fleeting of summer flowers. For a couple of weeks only, golf-ball-sized buds burst open into the most beautiful of garden flowers before high winds, rain or scorching midsummer sun wilts the petals and they drop as fast as they have opened.

PARTS USED

① Roots
② Flowers
③ Tree peony seeds (commerically harvested for edible oil)

Peonies may only open for a short time each year, but they've been on a very long journey to get to your garden and become the species they are today. You'll find peonies growing as trees, perennial plants, and forms that are a cross between the two, known as intersectional hybrids. These three forms of peony exist partly due to the plant's evolution during the course of its very long life – altering over 66 million years to adapt to changing terrains, climates and pollinators. We also have human cultivators to thank for peonies as we know them in our gardens today, especially the blousy, early summer perennial peony *lactiflora*.

In the Chinese, Greek and Roman Empires, wild peonies were used for a wide range of medicinal applications. Look to ancient Chinese artworks and Greek myths, and you will often encounter peony flowers in a starring role, revered for their medicinal prowess as well as their beauty. However, their flowers weren't the only parts of the plants that were held in high regard; their roots may be less beautiful, but were no less valuable to medics, and it was the medicinal properties of the roots (including their ability to detoxify the liver, reduce inflammation, clear blood, support gut health, reduce period cramps, calm stress and even improve memory) that made it a valuable trading plant over 2000 years ago. Known as *bao shao*, peony roots, like many traditional Chinese medicinal herbs, were often infused into nourishing broths as a way to access the benefits of the plant. In the spring the roots are still infused into simple vegetable soups with herbs like parsley and watercress to make a fortifying meal, or simmered with red dates and the honey-flavoured nashi (Chinese pear). If you're looking for flavours to pair with your peony, look to the other ingredients that peonies are paired with in Chinese medicine: pear, peach, ginger and liquorice are not only used together as medicinal allies, but also make wonderful flavour partners.

While the root has an earthy, herbal, bitter flavour and is mainly used to infuse into broths, the fleeting but abundant flowers are treated in a more frivolous way. The flowers themselves taste perfumed with a bitter tone, which is a perfect foil for sweet things. Peonies were traditionally sweetened with honey or poached for a moment in sugar syrups – just enough to balance the bitter perfume of the flower. Ground peony petals dusted onto sweet puddings and sweets balance their cloying flavour. Infused into pectin, they make summer jams that are reminiscent of the addictive bitter flavours of marmalade. If your tooth is less sweet, try dusting the petals in flour and frying them in sesame oil, or simply add them to mild salad leaves to create a delicious floral bowl that even the most discerning herb-munching dinosaur from peony's early days would have approved of.

SERVES 4

Peony and Spinach Salad with Raspberry Vinegar Dressing

Early summer heatwaves can come as a shock to our bodies that have been used to chill winds and thick jumpers. The first hot days see folk wilted and listless as they readjust to the heat. This is exactly when we need minimal effort meals that hydrate and cool as much as they nourish. As luck would have it, just as the heat of summer radiates from every corner, peony flowers burst open, providing a blink-and-you'll-miss-it display in the garden, in vases and in food. Their flowers have been used in cosmetics and Chinese herbal medicines for hydrating and cooling, and are the perfect bloom to add to this low-effort, maximum-taste salad.

1 peony flower
100g (3½ oz) baby leaf spinach, washed
1 red onion, thinly sliced
50 g (1¾ oz) goat's cheese

FOR THE DRESSING

100 g (3½ oz) raspberries
100 ml (3½ fl oz/scant ½ cup) extra virgin olive oil
50 ml (1¾ fl oz/3½ tbsp) red wine vinegar
25 g (¾ oz) sugar or light honey, to taste
salt and black pepper, to taste

For the dressing, place the raspberries in a small pan with a splash of water, set over a low heat and warm for a few minutes until they are broken apart and starting to reduce. Remove from the heat and press through a sieve over a bowl (you can use the leftover pulp on yoghurt or ice cream). Cool and whisk with the olive oil and vinegar, then taste for sweetness and add sugar to taste. Add a pinch of salt and a twist of ground pepper and leave the dressing to sit for an hour or so.

Meanwhile, pull the peony petals away from the flower head. If they are looking less than plump, plunge them into a bowl of room-temperature water for a couple of hours and they will absorb the water and plump back up. Mix the petals, spinach and onion together in a serving bowl, drizzle over the raspberry vinaigrette and crumble over the goat's cheese.

Serve in the shade next to a fan.

SERVES 4

Peaches Poached in Peony Petal and Vanilla Syrup

Peonies bloom as peaches ripen, and as serendipity often works peaches and peonies are perfect partners. A gentle poach of just-ripened peaches turn them into a stunning dessert with added benefits. The syrup left after the flower and fruit have soaked becomes a beautiful addition to summer drinks. Peony and peach Bellini, anyone?

- 500 ml (17 fl oz/2 cups) water
- 150 g (5 oz/⅔ cup) granulated sugar
- 4 just-ripe peaches, halved
- ½ vanilla pod
- pared zest of ½ lemon, plus 1 tsp juice
- 1 peony flower
- 300 ml (10 fl oz/1¼ cups) double (heavy) cream
- 6 amaretti biscuits, crumbled

Place the water and sugar in a pan and heat until all the sugar has dissolved and the liquid is clear. Turn the heat down and add the peach halves, cooking for a couple of minutes until they have only just started to soften. Remove from the heat and add the vanilla, lemon zest and most of the peony petals (reserving some for garnish). Cover the pan and allow the peaches to infuse in the floral syrup for 1 hour.

Remove the peaches with a slotted spoon and, if they're not too soft, slip off the skins, then place on a serving platter, cut-sides up.

Pour the cream into a mixing bowl and add a couple of tablespoons of the syrup along with the teaspoon of lemon juice. Whisk until it starts to thicken.

Spoon the cream on top of the peaches and serve scattered with the remaining peony flowers and crumbled amaretti biscuits.

The remaining peachy, bittersweet syrup is beautiful splashed into sparkling wine or served with puréed peaches and club soda as a non-alcoholic alternative to the Italian Bellini.

SERVES 4

Peony Root Soup

The dried roots of *Paeonia lactiflora* are a well-known herb in Chinese medicine (called *bai shao*), traditionally used as a revitalising herb for the skin as well as immune and mood-related conditions. Like many Chinese medicinal herbs, they are used in teas and broths, and add a nourishing earthy flavour to spring soups. This version of peony root soup infuses the root into water to make a stock, though you could add the root to a good-quality chicken or vegetable stock in place of the water to add further flavour and nutrition to this restorative bowl.

- 30 g (1 oz) white peony root
- 1 tsp light olive oil
- 2 leeks, finely chopped
- 3 celery sticks, finely chopped
- 2 garlic cloves, crushed
- ½ red chilli, finely diced
- thumb-sized piece of fresh root ginger, finely grated
- 200 g (7 oz/1¼ cups) green peas
- 1 tsp salt
- black pepper, to taste

TO SERVE

- 40 g (1½ oz) watercress, chopped
- 20 g (¾ oz) fresh parsley, chopped
- ½ pear, peeled, cored and sliced
- dried peony flowers, to gardish (optional)

Put the peony root in a saucepan, add 1 litre (34 fl oz/4 cups) water and simmer for 25 minutes.

Meanwhile, heat the olive oil in a large pan, then sweat the leeks, celery and garlic until soft.

Strain the root-infused water into the pan with the softened vegetables, then add the chilli and grated ginger. Simmer for a few minutes, then stir in the peas and simmer for a further 5 minutes, or until the peas are cooked. Add the salt and some black pepper, then taste and adjust to suit.

Serve hot or chilled, topped with the watercress, parsley, sliced pear and dried peony flowers, if using.

MAKES 12 PIECES

Peony Flower Fudge

Peony flowers are both bitter and creamy; infused into sweets, they make their sugary ingredients taste creamier and less sweet – the perfect antidote to tooth-curlingly sweet fudge.

450 g (1 lb/scant 2 cups) golden caster (superfine) sugar
400 ml (14 fl oz/generous 1½ cups) double (heavy) cream
50 g (1¾ oz) butter
1 tbsp glucose syrup
1 heaped tsp dried ground peony flowers (1 whole flower head will provide 1 heaped tsp)
salt, to taste

Melt the sugar, cream, butter and glucose syrup in a large saucepan, stirring to prevent the sugar from catching on the bottom of the pan. When the ingredients have dissolved, place a sugar thermometer into the pan and turn up the heat so that the mixture starts to boil and bubble. It will rise quite far up the pan so make sure your pan is not too small. Keep stirring the bubbling mixture until the sugar thermometer reads 116°C (241°F), a stage known as 'soft ball'. (If you don't have a sugar thermometer you can drop teaspoonfuls of the mixture into very cold water – if the mixture becomes like fudge, take it off the heat.) Remove from the heat and set aside until the thermometer reads 110°C (230°F). Once it is at this temperature, start mixing it as fast as you can with a wooden spoon until the fudge is thick and no longer glossy (it'll be around 60°C/140°F). Add three-quarters of the powdered peony flowers along with a small pinch of salt and keep beating the mixture for a few more minutes (if you stop before this you will have a crumbly, crunchy, tablet consistency).

Pour the fudge into a parchment-lined tupperware container, pressing it smooth. Brush a wet pastry brush over the surface and dust over the remaining powdered peony and another pinch of salt. Loosely cover with the lid and leave to cool for a few hours at room temperature before cutting into cubes to eat. The fudge will keep for up to 2 months in an airtight container.

SERVES 6 AS AN APERITIF

Peony and Liquorice Vermouth Cocktail

The combination of peony and liquorice is a pairing long known about in Chinese herbal medicine. A swirl of a liquorice sweet in a cocktail may not be medicinal, but it certainly is deliciously therapeutic. The creamy and bitter tones of peony flowers elevate a standard medium-sweet vermouth into a new realm, worthy of supping in the finest bars and gardens.

3 peony flowers
500 ml (17 fl oz/2 cups) bianco (blanc) vermouth (medium-sweet)
3 good-quality soft liquorice sweets, halved
cocktail skewers

Pull the peony petals from the flower head and pack them into a 500 ml (17 fl oz) jar. Fill the jar with vermouth, making sure the petals are pushed into the liquid. Leave to infuse for a couple of days before straining out the flowers.

To serve as an aperitif, serve 85 ml (3 fl oz/6 tbsp) over ice with half a liquorice sweet on a skewer. The sweet will start to dissolve and the liquorice flavour will permeate the vermouth. Once your vermouth is as liquorice as you would like it to be, enjoy the vermouth-soaked sweet with your drink.

You can also use the vermouth with soda, or gin to make yourself a peony Martini.

SERVES 10 GENEROUSLY

Peony Jam Sponge cake

Peonies make a beautiful jam: earthy, sweet and floral but with a bitterness like marmalade. Pairing them with sour apples not only creates a beautiful flavour, but the pectin in the fruit also helps the jam to set.

Light as air, fat-free sponges are the perfect bake to showcase the flavour and texture of this gorgeous peony jam. Fill with cream and serve chilled as a dessert with summer fruit or in dainty (but multiple) slices with high tea.

FOR THE JAM

1 kg (2 lb 4 oz) cooking apples (or sour apples like Granny Smiths)
juice of 1 lemon
2 fully opened peonies (without any blemishes)
granulated sugar (for quantity, see method)

FOR THE SPONGE

butter, for greasing
120 g (4 oz/1 cup) plain (all-purpose) flour, plus extra for dusting
4 eggs
120 g (4 oz/generous ½ cup) caster (superfine) sugar

TO SERVE

300 ml (10 fl oz/1¼ cups) whipped cream
20 g (¾ oz/2½ tbsp) icing (confectioners') sugar, for dusting
1 peony flower, to decorate

To make the pectin, wash and chop the whole apples (with the skin and cores) and place in a saucepan with the lemon juice. Cover with 1 litre (34 fl oz/4 cups) water and cook until the apple has completely collapsed. Add half of the peony petals, then remove from the heat and leave for a couple of hours before straining though a jelly bag or fine sieve lined with a muslin cloth into a measuring jug (don't press it through or you'll have cloudy pectin).

Measure and make a note of the amount of pectin you have made – it will inform the amount of sugar you now need to add. You will need three-quarters of the amount of sugar to pectin liquid (for example, if you have 400 ml/14 fl oz/generous 1½ cups pectin, add 300 g/ 10½ oz/1⅓ cups sugar).

Place a plate in the freezer to chill.

Place the pectin in a wide-based pan and warm before adding the sugar. Stir the mixture to make sure no sugar is stuck to the base of the pan and bring to the boil. The jam will become foamy; what's called a rolling boil. Keep boiling for a few minutes, then test to see whether it has reached setting point. Drip a few drops of the jam onto your cold plate; when it's ready, it will wrinkle when you push your finger through the jam.

When the jam has reached the setting point, turn off the heat and leave to cool slightly for 5 minutes before stirring in the remaining peony petals. Pour the jam into a couple of sterilised jam jars.

To make the sponge, preheat the oven to 180°C (350°F/gas 4). Grease a 20 cm (8 in) cake tin (pan) with butter and dust with flour.

Place the eggs and sugar into a heatproof mixing bowl set over a pan half-full of hot water over a low heat (ensure the base of the bowl does not touch the water). Whisk until the mixture becomes pale and doubles in size. Sift in the flour and gently fold until mixed throughout the light batter.

Pour the batter into the prepared cake tin and bake for 20–25 minutes until golden.

Remove from the oven and cool the sponge on a wire rack before slicing in half and filling with the peony jam and a generous amount of whipped cream. Dust with icing sugar and decorate with peony flower.

FLAVOUR PROFILE Citrus-Lemony · Sweet · Green · Bitter · Minty

Lavender

COMMONLY USED EDIBLE SPECIES

Lavandula angustifolia (English lavender) varieties.

WHERE THEY GROW

Lavender thrives in full sun, in well-drained, poor soil.

WHEN TO GATHER

Young stems – spring onwards

Flowers – summer

PARTS USED

① Young leaf stems
② Flowers

When Howard Carter discovered Pharaoh Tutankhamun's tomb in 1922, he found lavender in it that was so perfectly preserved that he claimed he could smell its fragrance 3,000 years after it had been placed in the burial chamber. (Had I been in the group of explorers, the discovery of 3,000-year-old lavender would have been far more exciting than the mummified pharaoh.) The pharaoh would have also been wrapped in clothes drenched in lavender oil when he was embalmed, in a ritual that aimed to preserve the deceased, because a well-preserved, perfumed body was far more likely to make the grade into the afterlife (and rightly so). His death probably wouldn't have been the first time Tutankhamun smelt of lavender, as by the time he ruled over Egypt, the flower was widely used amongst the living as well as the dead in cosmetics, massage oils, medicines, perfumes and to wash bodies and clothes (hence the name lavender, which comes from *lavo*, meaning 'to wash'). If you have a lavender-scented laundry powder, you're following in ancient perfumed footsteps.

Just like the fragrant ancient tombs, lavender probably scents your modern-day garden – the shrubby plant is one of the most commonly grown herbs. Even in the hands of the least green-fingered gardener and in neglected, sun-baked soils, lavender will thrive alongside its aromatic mint family siblings – rosemary, thyme, sage and oregano. Whilst its relatives may be more familiar now in the kitchen, all of these aromatic, woody herbs started being planted in gardens more for their medicinal value: thyme for bacterial infections, rosemary for circulation, sage for sore throats, oregano for coughs and lavender for almost everything else (headaches, stress, exhaustion, infections, muscle aches, washing and healing wounds. In fact, soldiers from the Roman Empire all the way up until the First World War carried lavender as a first aid herb for wounds.)

The other herbs, with their savoury gentle flavours, slowly moved from medicinal flower beds into kitchen herb gardens, and are today better known as culinary herbs, leaving lavender behind, unsure of whether it belonged in the kitchen or in the apothecary. In truth, it belongs in both, but its medicinal powers and beautiful perfume that are so revered came with a cost – like the child who doesn't know his own strength, lavender has an almost brutish flavour if not handled with care. Too much lavender can overpower a dish, making it bitter and inedible, but a tiny sprinkle can lift the flavour of fruits, cut through the fattiness of meats, add layers of flavour to floury grains and send preserves into other heavenly realms (along with lavender-scented pharaohs).

How to tame that perfumed beast? The first step in successful flavouring with lavender is to select the right species – and that species is *Lavandula angustifolia*, commonly known as English lavender (rather confusingly, because this lavender hails from the mountains of the Mediterranean). English lavender has a sweeter, more rosemary-like flavour than the French and Spanish varieties, which are much stronger and are best used for essential oils and perfumes.

Once you've selected the right lavender, you can harvest it before the flowers even open – the green, new, tender shoots are almost lemony and make a beautiful flavouring from mid-spring onwards. Lavender stalks chopped finely, add a light and fresh, almost zesty flavour when sprinkled onto salads and baked cheeses like sharp fetas.

Once the flowers are opening, use them fresh or dried (you can dry your flowers by hanging long stems in loose bundles in a warm place – keep a large bowl under them to catch any seeds as they fall to sow in seed trays for future harvests and you'll be a lavender-eating flower farmer in no time!). Just be aware that lavender flowers become more concentrated when you dry them – a good rule is to use a third of the quantity of dried flowers to fresh.

Once you've harvested and dried your flowers, you've got a flavouring so intense it needs huge respect and nimble fingers. Lavender, like jasmine, is best infused into a carrier of flavour, giving you more control over how much you're adding to a dish. A harvest of lavender flowers infused into a jar of sugar (much like lilac sugar), blended into sea salt, olive oil, or with its historical herb allies makes it a far easier flavour to tame and to cook with, giving you the merest wisp of beautiful perfume rather than something so potent you can sense it, like Howard Carter did 3,000 years later.

SERVES 4

Lavender Herb Blend with Pork, Apple and Dumplings

Due to its ability to overpower a meal if too much is used, lavender is a lesser-spotted ingredient in main-course dishes, but with a delicate hand, it can elevate even the most savoury of foods. The trick is in ensuring that you don't sprinkle a flower bud too many, and making use of its more savoury cousins from the mint family. Jars of ready-blended herbs, with just the right amount of lavender in them, mean you no longer have to play over-seasoning roulette. It is worth making a few jars, as they will soon be emptied – pinched into a pan of white beans, onions, into burger and sausage mixes, sprinkled over focaccia dough, or onto pork for the most beautiful of roast cracklings. Make sure you make enough to keep you stocked through the winter when casseroles and dumplings are the order of the day, as lavender turns them into the ultimate comfort food.

FOR THE LAVENDER HERB BLEND

2 tsp dried rosemary
2 tsp dried thyme
2 tsp dried savory
1 tsp dried lovage
1 tsp dried hyssop
½ tsp dried lavender

FOR THE PORK AND APPLE CASSEROLE

20 g (¾ oz) butter
good glug of olive oil
1 large onion, thickly sliced
500g (1 lb 2 oz) diced pork
1 tbsp plain (all-purpose) flour
250 ml (8½ fl oz/1 cup) chicken stock
300 ml (10 fl oz/1¼ cups) cider or sharp apple juice
50 ml (1¾ fl oz/3 tbsp) single (light) cream
1 large russet apple (or other that keeps its shape when cooked), thinly sliced
1 garlic clove, crushed

FOR THE DUMPLINGS

140 g (5 oz) suet
250 g (9 oz/2 cups) self-raising flour
½ tsp baking powder
1 tsp lavender herb blend (see above)
1 tsp English mustard
pinch of salt

For the herb blend, just mix together the dried herbs and store in an airtight jar for up to 12 months.

Preheat the oven to 180°C (350°F/gas 4).

For the pork and apple casserole, melt the butter with the olive oil in a flameproof casserole dish (Dutch oven) that has a tight-fitting lid over a medium-high heat. Add the onion and sweat until it becomes translucent, then add the garlic and cook for a few minutes before adding the pork pieces and cook until they start to colour. Reduce the heat and coat the meat and onions with the flour, scraping the base of the dish with a wooden spoon to lift up anything that sticks. Once fully coated, pour over the chicken stock and cider/apple juice, and cook for 10 minutes over a low heat. Remove from heat and stir in the cream, then add the sliced apple and set aside.

To make the dumplings, rub together the suet, flour, baking powder, lavender herb blend, mustard and salt, adding enough cold water to form a very soft dough. Lightly form the mixture into walnut-sized dumplings, making sure not to overwork the dough. Place the dumplings on top of the pork and apple casserole, cover with the lid and place the oven for 25 minutes, removing the lid for the final 5 minutes.

Serve with leafy green vegetables (perhaps only telling any lavender cynics what they've eaten when they have inevitably licked the plate clean).

MAKES 20

Lavender Salt and Lemon Zest Biscuits

The slight bitterness in lavender is a delicious foil for buttery sweet biscuits. Making a double batch means you can freeze one ready to slice should you have an unexpected guest (or an unexpected craving).

FOR THE LAVENDER SALT

1 tbsp lavender flowers
75 g (2½ oz/generous ½ cup) sea salt flakes

FOR THE BISCUITS

150 g (5½ oz/scant ¾ cup) unsalted butter (room temperature)
120 g (4¼ oz/1 cup) caster (superfine) sugar
½ tsp lavender salt (plus a pinch to sprinkle over the biscuits)
zest of 1 lemon
220 g (8 oz/1 cup) plain (all-purpose) flour
3 egg yolks, beaten

To make the lavender salt, grind the flowers and salt together in a pestle and mortar until the salt becomes slightly damp and the flowers are broken up. Add a small splash of water and mix in (the water will help the salt absorb the flavour of the lavender). Spread the salt over a dish and place above a warm radiator or in a dehydrator to evaporate the excess water.

Once dry, spoon the salt into a jar, where it will keep for up to 6 months.

For the biscuits, beat the butter and sugar together until light and fluffy. Mix in the lavender salt and lemon zest before stirring in a spoonful of the flour. Add two-thirds of the beaten yolks (the rest is to glaze the biscuits) and the rest of the flour, mixing until you have a smooth dough. Roll the dough into a 25-cm (10-in) long sausage; wrap in grease proof paper and place in the refrigerator for 1 hour (or freeze).

Using a bread knife, slice the chilled dough into 20 pieces, placing each slice on a lined baking tray; chill for a further 10 minutes before glazing with the remaining egg yolk.

Bake in an oven preheated to 175°C (325°F/gas 3) for 12 minutes, until golden. Remove from the oven and sprinkle with a pinch of the lavender salt.

MAKES
4 × 150 ML
(5 FL OZ)
JARS

Lavender and Apple Jelly

Apple and lavender jelly is sweet enough to slather on scones but with enough savoury bite to be a perfect condiment for cheese boards and roast dinners. If you haven't had jelly and cheese before, now is the time to leap straight in and discover quite how marvellous it is.

Lavender is beautiful by itself, but if you happen to have sorrel in your garden, a cup of finely shredded leaves brings a wonderful acidity to the jelly.

- 2 kg (4lb 8 oz) cooking apples (or crab apples)
- juice of 1 lemon
- 10 flowering lavender stems (flowers and stems)
- 450 g (1 lb/4½ cups) granulated sugar
- 100 ml (3½ fl oz/scant ½ cup) cider vinegar
- 25 g (¾ oz) sorrel, finely shredded (optional)

Wash and chop the whole apples along with the skin and cores. Place in a saucepan with the lemon juice, cover with 1 litre (34 fl oz/4 cups) water and cook until the apple becomes fluffy and soft (this usually takes around 15 minutes). Remove from the heat and stir in the lavender flowers and stems. Leave for a couple of hours to infuse, then strain through a fine muslin-lined sieve into a measuring jug (don't press it through or you'll have a cloudy pectin mixture).

Place a plate in the freezer to chill.

Measure 600 ml (20 fl oz/2½ cups) of your apple pectin into a deep, wide-based pan and warm the liquid before adding the sugar and vinegar. Stir the mixture to make sure no sugar is stuck to the base of the pan and bring to the boil. The jelly will become foamy; what's called a rolling boil. Keep boiling for a few minutes, then test to see whether it has reached setting point. Drip a few drops of the jelly onto your cold plate; when it's ready, it will wrinkle when you push your finger through the jelly.

When the jelly has reached the setting point, turn off the heat and leave to cool slightly for 5 minutes before stirring in a few lavender flowers. If you are adding sorrel, stir it in now. Pour the jelly into sterilised jam jars and store in the refrigerator for up to 3 months.

SERVES 4–6

Butterflied Lamb Marinated in Lavender, Oregano and Mint

Square-stemmed, aromatic lavender, thyme, oregano and mint are all siblings in the mint family. They get along incredibly well in oil marinades for barbecuing meat like lamb. This marinade is also beautiful used to preserve cubes of salty feta, or even to brush liberally on the cheese with a drizzle of honey before it is roasted.

1 butterflied lamb leg weighing 2 kg (4 lb 8 oz), (ask your butcher to prepare this for you)

FOR THE MARINADE

4 stems of lavender, flowers chopped
2 tsp of oregano, leaves finely chopped
2 tsp of thyme, leaves finely chopped
2 stems of mint, leaves chopped
zest of ¼ lemon (retain the lemon for the next day)
1 garlic clove
pinch of salt
pinch of freshly ground black pepper
pinch of chilli (red pepper) flakes
150 ml (5 fl oz/scant ⅔ cup) olive oil

Place all the marinade ingredients, except the oil, into a large pestle and mortar, and pound until the garlic and herbs are broken up. Mix with the oil.

Rub half of the marinade all over the lamb, place the lamb in a large container or ziplock bag and refrigerate overnight.

The next day, bring out the lamb a couple of hours before cooking so that the meat can return to room temperature.

If oven-cooking, preheat the oven to 180°C (350°F/gas 4).

If you are barbecuing the meat, place it on a hot part of the barbecue for a few minutes to brown the meat, then move it to a cooler part of the barbecue (you can adjust the temperature of parts of the barbecue by moving your charcoal to different areas). Cook for around 20 minutes, basting the lamb with the leftover marinade.

If oven-cooking, brown the meat all over in a frying pan (skillet) first before roasting in the oven for 15–20 minutes.

Once the lamb is cooked to your preference, remove from the barbecue/oven and let it rest for 15 minutes. Squeeze the juice from the zested lemon over the meat and serve with a feta-and-mint-laden green salad.

MAKES 12 SLICES

Lavender, Pear and Almond Cake

The citrus hint in lavender that comes courtesy of the aromatic compound linalool is a perfect addition to Italian pear and almond cakes. And any leftover pear and lavender syrup could come to a far worse ending than being poured into a Champagne glass with a chilled sparkling wine as a fragrant twist on a Perry cocktail.

FOR THE LAVENDER SYRUP

- 400 ml (14 fl oz/generous 1½ cups) boiling water
- 200 g (7 oz/scant 1 cup) caster (superfine) sugar
- zest and juice of ½ lemon
- 1 tsp dried or 3 tsp fresh lavender flowers

FOR THE CAKE

- 6 ripe but firm pears
- 125 g (4½ oz) softened butter (if using unsalted butter, add a pinch of salt to the flour)
- 125 g (4½ oz/generous ½ cup) caster (superfine) sugar
- 2 large eggs
- 90 g (3¼ oz/¾ cup) self-raising flour
- 125 g (4½ oz/1¼ cups) ground almonds
- 100 g (3½ oz/generous 1 cup) flaked (slivered) almonds

To make the syrup, pour the boiling water over the sugar and stir until the sugar is dissolved. Add the lemon zest and juice along with the lavender flowers, and leave to infuse while you prepare the pears.

Peel and halve the pears from top to bottom, then use a sharp knife to cut out the cores and the fibrous strands that run up to the stems, retaining the peel and cores for later. Lay the pears in a baking dish, pour over the lavender-infused syrup, and leave to soak for at least 1 hour.

Preheat the oven to 190°C (375°F/gas 5).

Meanwhile, make the batter. Beat together the butter and sugar until creamy, then beat in the eggs one at a time before slowly adding the flour and ground almonds, mixing gently until the cake batter is smooth.

Spoon the batter into a 20 cm (8 in) springform or loose-bottomed cake tin (pan). Place the pear halves into the cake batter, positioning the narrowest part of the pear in the centre, so that the halves form a shape that looks like the spokes of a wheel.

Bake for 25 minutes, or until the top of the cake is turning light golden and springs back when pressed.

Meanwhile, put the reserved pear peelings and cores in a pan with the syrup that the pears were soaking in, set over a low heat and simmer until the syrup is slightly reduced. Strain into a jug. Place the flaked almonds in a bowl and pour over enough of the syrup to coat them, stirring to make sure all of the nuts are sticky.

Scatter the syrupy flaked almonds over the top of the cake and place it back into the oven for a few minutes until the almonds start to turn slightly golden.

Remove from the oven and serve hot or cold with a drizzle of the pear and lavender syrup.

FLAVOUR PROFILE Aromatic · Thyme · Oregano · Mint · Lavender ·Earl Grey Tea

Bee Balm

COMMONLY USED EDIBLE SPECIES

Monarda fistulosa (wild bergamot/bee balm), *Monarda didyma* (scarlet bee balm), *Monarda citriodora* (lemon bee balm).

WHERE THEY GROW

Bee balms grow best in full sun, with space between the plants for air to circulate and prevent powdery mildew.

WHEN TO GATHER

From mid-spring until late summer.

PARTS USED

① Flowers
② Leaves

You might know bee balm as wild bergamot, or by its scientific, botanical name of *Monarda didyma*. Botanical names are regarded as a plant's correct name, which spell out its family and individual species. They were introduced by Swedish naturalist Carl Linnaeus in the 1700s who developed the now globally recognised way of naming plants. His system has lots of benefits, including, perhaps most importantly, giving plants unique, globally recognised names, which helps differentiate them from other species with the same name in different locations. For example, your sorrel might be a shrub, *Hibiscus rosa-sinensis*, whereas mine is a little grassland plant, *Rumex acetosa*. But those other, 'common' or local names often came from the communities who had lived alongside the plants for thousands of years. Whilst the scientific naming of plants is incredibly useful for identifying specific species, it has a tendency to diminish its older names and whitewash the plant's history – playing down the value it had to the people the plants belonged to before they were swept up into European hands.

Bee balms had just one of those long histories: used for thousands of years in food and medicine, to treat, amongst other things, bee stings. This family of plants, now known as *Monardas*, grows wild across its native homeland of North America. And just as America was renamed in the 16th century after Italian Amerigo Vespucci, so bee balms were rechristened in honour of Spanish botanist Nicolas Monardes, who – unlike Vespucci – never even visited the continent, let alone saw its beautiful bee balms in situ.

Bee balm (as we shall call it) and its siblings have their own unique characteristics and flavours, which are captured perfectly by their non-botanical names: bee balms soothe stings; lemon bee balm leaves no room to speculate which citrus fruit it tastes of; while wild bee balms (*Monarda fistulosa*) are also known by the names sweetleaf and wild oregano, which provide a pretty accurate guide to their flavours.

Nicolas Monardes himself gave scarlet bee balm another name based on its smell and flavour. Its Latin name *didyma* described the pairs of stamens the flower has, but his other name for the plant, *Monarda* bergamot came from the way that those same flowers smelt of bergamot fruit (whose peel was added to Earl Grey tea). Back in America, bee balm was also known for its tea association, but was named Oswego tea, after the Oswego people of what is now New York state, who used the plant in herbal brews long before Europeans with their bone china tea sets arrived on the continent's shores.

In an almost ridiculous twist of fate, Oswego tea was one of the alternatives to the traditional camellia leaf that the European settlers themselves drank after they pushed chests of it into the Boston Harbour in 1773, as an act of protest against the Tea Act imposed by Britain, in cahoots with one of the biggest beneficiaries of colonisation – the British East India Company. You no doubt know that pushing the tea into the harbour eventually led to the American Revolution and the country's independence from Britain, which left a continent named after an Italian, full of plants renamed by a Swede in honour of a Spaniard.

Wherever you are in the world, whatever name you choose to use for your plants – Oswego tea, bee balm, *Monarda didyma* or wild bergamot – take a moment to think back to the plant's roots and historical uses and it'll become far more useful than simply ornamental. Not only did the Oswego people drink their sweet bee balm as tea and use it as a medicine, it was also used to flavour food – its leaves and flowers used like oregano as a herb: fresh in salads in the spring and summer, and dried as a warming aromatic herb in stews and soups in the colder months. And remember, botanical names may be useful, but to properly understand a plant, you need to find out what it's really called.

SERVES 4

Roast Squash with Bee Balm and Feta

Bee balm and squashes both hail from the Americas. Bee balm started its journey in the North, in the foothills of the Rocky Mountains, slowly spreading east and west. Pumpkins and squashes on the other hand, first started life in the south of the continent. Both wended their ways being used as medicine and food by the Indigenous peoples until at some point in time their paths would have met. Pumpkin and bee balm's close cousin oregano make such an iconic flavour pairing that it wouldn't be too far-fetched to think that perhaps they were cooked with each other thousands of years ago, way before both plants were transported to Europe, where the squashes were planted in vegetable gardens and bee balms in ornamental beds. Whether they were eaten together in the distant past or not, bee balm and squashes bring out the best of each other's flavours, especially when roasted and served with a sharp feta and the crunch of toasted pumpkin seeds.

1 medium squash or small pumpkin (butternuts are ideal)
2 tbsp olive oil
salt, to taste
large handful or 15 g (½ oz) dried bee balm leaves and flowers
100 g (3½ oz) feta

Preheat the oven to 220°C (425°F/gas 7).

Cut the squash into slices, reserving the seeds. Toss the slices in most of the olive oil and season with salt before laying on a roasting tray (pan).

Rinse the squash seeds and coat in the remaining olive oil, season with salt and arrange in a single layer in another roasting tray.

Roast both trays in the oven for 20 minutes. After 20 minutes, remove the seeds if they are golden. Turn the squash slices over and return them to the oven for another 10 minutes, or until caramelised on the edges.

Meanwhile, place the roasted seeds and most of the dried bee balm in a spice grinder and blend until the seeds are broken up into a crunchy texture, adding salt to season.

Remove the pumpkin slices from the oven and place in a serving dish. Crumble over the feta, the pumpkin seed mix and the remaining dried bee balm. Serve as a side dish or as a main course with a grain salad. Any leftovers can be puréed with stock and turned into soup, or mashed and stirred through fried gnocchi or pasta.

SERVES 4

Cabbage Slaw with Bee Balm Oxymel

Oxymels are ancient herbal medicinal preparations made by infusing herbs in honey and vinegar. A bee balm oxymel will preserve the potent, immune-boosting, antimicrobial properties of the herb for when it is out of season. This little bit of effort in making an oxymel will repay you well because not only will you be able to add another medicine to your home apothecary, you'll also have made a delicious store-cupboard flavouring to dress salads and turn into drinks.

FOR THE OXYMEL

- 500 ml (17 fl oz/generous 2 cups) jar filled with fresh or dried chopped bee balm
- 250 ml (8½ fl oz/1 cup) honey (ideally raw, as it gives the biggest benefits)
- 250 ml (8½ fl oz/1 cup) unpasteurised apple cider vinegar, plus (optional) extra to serve

FOR THE SLAW

- ½ red cabbage
- 1 large carrot
- ½ large red onion
- ½ green chilli
- salt, to taste
- handful of fresh bee balm leaves and flowers, finely chopped

For the oxymel, place the chopped bee balm in a jar with a non-corrosive lid (a 1-litre jar with a rubber seal is ideal). Add the honey and apple cider vinegar, using a fork to press the herbs down into it to help any air bubbles escape. The flavour of the bee balm will start to infuse into the sweetened vinegar almost immediately. If you want to use the dressing straight away, leave it to infuse for 1 hour, stirring regularly to mix the honey and vinegar together. Decant as much as you'd like to use, before topping up with more honey and vinegar. Otherwise, leave the mixture to absorb the properties of the plant for a few weeks before straining.

For the slaw, finely shred the cabbage, carrot and onion, and very finely dice the green chilli. Combine in a bowl and sprinkle with a pinch of salt. Pour over 50 ml (1¾ fl oz/3 tablespoons) of strained oxymel and toss well to combine. Taste and add a splash more vinegar if too sweet, or an extra pinch of salt if needed. Leave to marinate for at least 1 hour before serving.

When ready to serve, top the slaw with the chopped bee balm leaves and flowers. As all slaws are, this is absolutely delicious served with a barbecue.

SERVES 2

Bee Balm, Oregano and Thyme Salad

In Lebanon, oregano and thyme are used as much as salad herbs as for flavouring food. Removed from their woody stalks, the small, pungent leaves make beautiful salads to accompany *meze* dishes. Bee balm's young leaves sit somewhere between thyme and oregano in flavour, and like their mint siblings, taste delicious as a salad leaf. This dish is great served with grilled meats and flatbreads, as it is or with feta crumbled on top.

1 onion, finely sliced
50 g (1¾ oz) of a mixture of fresh bee balm, thyme and oregano leaves
60 ml (2 fl oz/¼ cup) olive oil
120 ml (4 fl oz/½ cup) lemon juice
1 tsp sumac
salt and black pepper, to taste

Soak the sliced onion in a bowl of water for 15 minutes to mellow the flavour. Drain and pat dry on paper towels.

Meanwhile, wash the herb stalks and, holding them like a bunch of flowers, shake thoroughly to dry. Separate the leaves from the stalks and place the leaves into a mixing bowl with the sliced onion, olive oil, lemon juice and sumac. Add salt and pepper to taste, then toss the salad together. Let the salad sit for a while to blend the flavours before serving.

MAKES
A 900 G
(2 LB) LOAF

Bee Balm Tea Bread

Soaking dried fruits in leftover tea makes exceptional use of the tannic drink, plumping and sweetening the fruit, which in turn makes fruit breads so delicious that whole nations pin their identities on them. *Bara brith*, for example, is one of the most beloved and fiercely protected Welsh fruit cakes. This tea bread is more of an internationalist, influenced by *bara brith* and Irish *barmbrack*, but flavoured with American bee balm – a proudly influenced cake.

250 ml (8½ fl oz/1 cup) strong, hot black tea
450 g (1 lb) dried fruit (sultanas/golden raisins, currants and raisins)
6 stems of bee balm
pared zest of 1 unwaxed orange
butter or oil, for greasing
1 egg
200 g (7 oz/1⅔ cup) plain (all-purpose) flour, sifted
200 g (7 oz/generous 1 cup) light brown sugar
1 tsp baking powder

Brew the tea. Place the dried fruit in a large heatproof bowl and pour over the tea along with enough just-boiled water to cover all the fruit. Remove any flower heads from the bee balm and set aside, then break the stems so that they can fit in among the soaking fruit. Add the stems with their leaves and the orange zest, cover and leave overnight for the fruit to plump up and absorb the tea and bee balm flavours.

The next day, preheat the oven to 150°C (300°F/gas 2). Grease and line a 900 g (2 lb) loaf tin (pan).

Strain the fruit and remove the bee balm stems and orange zest. Place the fruit into a mixing bowl and stir in the egg and add any bee balm flowers you reserved, separating the trumpet-like petals (if you don't have any flowers, that's okay).

In a separate bowl, sift together the flour, sugar and baking powder, then add in batches to the fruit mixture, gently folding the wet and dry ingredients together. Pour the mixture into the prepared loaf tin and bake for 1½ hours, or until a skewer comes out clean when pushed into the middle of the bread. Cool on a wire rack.

Serve sliced with slabs of salted butter, slithers of cheese and copious pots of tea (bee balm or otherwise).

SERVES 4

Bee Balm Ice Cream

If you were in any doubt about whether oregano-flavoured bee balm was a good thing with which to flavour ice cream, just eat a nectar-rich, sweet but deeply herbal bee balm flower and all of your doubts will be soothed away. Aromatic herbs are a perfectly grown-up foil for sweet ice cream, served with late-summer blackberries or alongside a cup of coffee at the end of a meal. It'll not so much cleanse your palate as fill it with a delicious reminder that herbal ice cream is worth planting bee balm for.

- 300 ml (10 fl oz/1¼ cups) whole milk
- 300 ml (10 fl oz/1¼ cups) double (heavy) cream
- 100 g (3½ oz/scant ½ cup) caster (superfine) sugar
- 5 g (¼ oz) dried bee balm leaves
- 4 egg yolks
- maple syrup or runny honey, to serve
- sea salt flakes, to serve
- dried bee balm petals, to garnish

Gently warm the milk and cream in a pan, add the sugar and stir until the grains have dissolved. Add the bee balm leaves to the mixture and leave to steep and cool for at least 30 minutes. Taste the mixture to check that the bee balm's herbal flavour has infused into the cream.

Beat the egg yolks in a large jug. Place a strainer above the jug and pour the infused cream and milk mixture over the eggs. Stir well and pour back into the pan (making sure to remove any remaining pieces of herb).

Place the pan back over the heat and, stirring continually, heat until the mixture starts to thicken into a loose custard (make sure to scrape the bottom of the pan to prevent the mixture from catching). Once thick, remove the pan from the heat and place a snugly fitting circle of greaseproof paper on the top of the custard (this will stop it forming a skin as it cools).

Once cool, transfer the custard to an ice-cream machine and churn until set. (Alternatively, pour the mixture into a tupperware container and place in the freezer for a couple of hours before removing and whipping with an electric whisk. Place back in the freezer and repeat this process until the ice cream is smooth and frozen.)

Serve in little bowls with a drizzle of maple syrup or runny honey and a tiny sprinkle of sea salt flakes and dried bee balm petals.

FLAVOUR PROFILE Water lily stems and flowers are mild tasting, the seeds are earthy, nutty and slightly peppery.

Water Lily

COMMONLY USED EDIBLE SPECIES

Nymphaea odorata (American water lily), *Nymphaea pubescens* (hairy water lily), *Euryale ferox* (prickly water lily – produces seeds sold as fox nuts/*makhana*), *Nuphar polysepala* (yellow water lily).

WHERE THEY GROW

Water lilies can be grown in ponds – they need to be planted in areas with full sun in order to flower. Various cultivars suit different pond depths and sizes.

WHEN TO GATHER

Early summer to autumn (fall)

If you flew over the Mekong Delta during the water lily harvest, you'd look down on the most incredible sight: swaying mandalas of green spokes tipped with fuchsia pinks, drifting around people as they wade in chest-deep water to pull up the flowering stems, collecting the new growth. The lily flowers and their long thick stems may look stunning floating around their gatherers, but they're being harvested for practical rather than ornamental reasons – namely, to be eaten. Water lilies, like the rice that grows in flooded paddy fields, and watercress that flourishes in chalk streams, and numerous other edible aquatic plants, are rich in nutrients. They are an invaluable, sustainable food resource for anyone living in flooded lands and beyond.

PARTS USED

① Shoots
② Leaves
③ Leaf stems
④ Flowers
⑤ Rhizomes (only from certain species)

CAUTION

Some edible species of water lily have inedible parts, such as tubers. Always check which parts are edible in your species. Soak and cook water lilies prior to use.

Species of water lily aren't just eaten in Southeast Asia, but in continents as diverse as North and South America, Africa and Australia. Like its aquatic neighbour, the lotus, water lily rhizomes are full of starches – an important source of carbohydrates in a watery landscape. Species with edible roots can be thinly sliced and cooked as a vegetable or roasted as they are in Africa. Drying and grinding the roots makes a flour like arrowroot or cornflour (cornstarch) that is used to thicken soups and stews.

From the roots, thick stems full of air chambers grow up to the surface of the water, topped with waxy leaves complete with their characteristic notches cut out like a slice of cake. These stems and the leaves are as nutritious as the roots – peel away the thin waterproof skin like you'd peel rhubarb, and you can snap the stem into bite-size pieces, soak them in clean water before cooking in curries and stir-fries. Dotted amongst the leaves are the iconic flowers. Ranging from pink to white, they can be harvested to make pakoras, to be paired with dips made from water-loving mint or watercress they're the aquatic fritter to beat all others.

However, don't be tempted to collect all of the flowers because you'll miss out on a final feast. Once the blooms have pollinated, they sink back under the water to grow into fruits full of seeds, which, if left to their own devices, will float away when ripe to form a new plant. In Bangladesh and India, the fruits are gathered and, though some species are eaten raw, more often the seeds are removed from the fruit and fried in ghee or oil until they pop like corn – rich in protein and minerals, water lily seeds are eaten as a snack with spices, sweetened with jaggery, or ground up into a nutritious powder to thicken puddings like kheer.

In cultures where water lilies aren't historically eaten the plant is often associated with signs of poverty, seen as a food that people would only eat because they had to rather than chose to. Little did the people who made those claims know that this aquatic edible is nourishing, nutritious, delicious and just so happens to also be one of the most beautiful and sustainable of harvests we have in the world. At a time when rising water levels and flooding are affecting more and more parts of the world, perhaps the beautiful water lily and its underwater crop can be considered a future food.

SERVES 4

Water Lily Flower Pakoras

Across the Indian Delta, water lily flowers and stems are dipped in batters and served as pakoras and fritters. If you don't have many flowers, you can fritter the stems, line up six 5-cm (2-in) lengths of stem and pierce them with a couple of skewers (they'll look like mini rafts), dip in batter and fry before removing the skewers.

FOR THE PAKORAS

45 g (1¾ oz/generous ⅓ cup) chickpea (gram) flour
10 g (½ oz/1 tbsp) rice flour
½ tsp nigella seeds
¼ tsp ground turmeric
large pinch of chilli powder
good pinch of salt
100 ml (3½ fl oz/scant ½ cup) water
12 water lily flowers
1 litre (34 fl oz/4¼ cups) vegetable oil, for frying
¼ tsp baking powder

FOR THE MINT YOGHURT

5 g (¼ oz/¼ cup) mint leaves, plus extra to serve
5 g (¼ oz/¼ cup) coriander (cilantro) leaves
1 green chilli, roughly chopped
juice of ½ lime
½ tsp caster (superfine) sugar
pinch of salt
¼ tsp ground cumin
200ml (7 fl oz/scant 1 cup) plain yoghurt

To make the mint yoghurt, blend all of the ingredients apart from the yoghurt to a paste in a food processor. Mix the herb paste into the yoghurt, adding a splash of water if the dip is too thick. Cover with a piece of baking parchment and refrigerate until the pakoras are ready to eat.

For the pakoras, mix together the flours, spices and salt with the water (adding more if needed) to create a thick, but pourable batter. Set aside to rest for 30 minutes.

Prepare the water lily flowers by removing any translucent, damaged petals.

Heat the oil in a pan to 180°C (350°F).

Just before frying, stir the baking powder into the batter. Plunge the flowers into the batter mix before carefully placing them in batches into the hot oil. Fry until dark golden, then remove with a slotted spoon to drain on paper towels.

Serve immediately with the mint yoghurt, topped with some finely chopped mint leaves.

SERVES 4

Water Lily Stem Noodle Broth

Water lilies grow fast in the fertile fresh water of Southeast Asia and are as linked to food in the frequently flooded region as are other aquatic edible plants, such as rice, and water chestnuts. Perhaps fittingly, having spent life growing under water, water lily stems are often served swimming in spiced broths. This noodle broth recipe is inspired by *nom banh*, a Cambodian breakfast bowl of noodles, fish, beansprouts, cucumber and water lily in coconut milk.

- 10 water lily stems
- salt, for the soaking water
- 1–2 bird's eye chillies
- 4 garlic cloves
- thumb-sized piece of fresh root ginger
- 2 lemongrass stalks
- 8 lime leaves
- handful of coriander (cilantro), stalks and leaves separated
- splash of vegetable oil
- 1 litre (34 fl oz/4¼ cups) vegetable or chicken stock
- 400 ml (14 fl oz) tinned coconut milk
- 200 g (7 oz) cherry tomatoes
- juice of 1 lime
- 2 tbsp fish sauce (or vegetarian alternative)

TO SERVE

- 200g (7 oz) fine rice noodles, cooked
- thinly sliced cucumber or sugar snap peas
- handful of mint leaves, roughly chopped (Vietnamese mint if possible)
- handful of basil leaves, roughly chopped (Thai basil if possible)
- edible flowers, such as viola, nasturtium or begonia (pictured), to garnish

Wash the water lily stems and peel away the thin outer layer (like the skin on a rhubarb stalk). Slice the stems lengthways, cutting them into fine, noodle-thin strips, ideally through the hollow tubes that run up the stems (these can collect grit and sand from the water they grow in and cutting them open helps to wash it out). Chop the fine strands up into 5 cm (2 in) lengths and soak in salted water until needed.

Combine the chillies, garlic, ginger, lemongrass and lime leaves with the coriander stems (reserve the leaves for serving) and vegetable oil in a food processor and blend to a paste.

Transfer the paste to a saucepan and cook for a couple of minutes, stirring all the time to ensure it doesn't burn. Pour in the stock and coconut milk, stir well and bring to the boil before turning the pan down to a gentle simmer. Add the tomatoes, lime juice and fish sauce, and simmer for 10 minutes, then add the prepared lily stems and cook for a couple more minutes to soften the stems slightly.

Place a pile of cooked noodles in the bottom of a serving bowl, pour the sauce over and top with slices of cucumber or sugar snap peas, roughly chopped coriander leaves, mint and basil, and edible flowers (if you have a water lily, use the petals of the flower, too). Serve.

SERVES 4

Spiced Water Lily Seeds

Water lily seeds are rich in minerals and protein. The seeds are harvested from a species known as the prickly water lily, which grows across the waterways of south and east Asia, the seeds forming in seed pods under the large, spiny lily pads. If you don't have an abundant seeding water lily in your water course, you can buy *phool makhana* (or fox nuts) from a wide range of online shops. Whilst this is a delicious snack in itself, infused with the fruity, spiced flavours of chaat masala, you can add nuts, shavings of coconut, dried fruit and other spices to make your own unique water lily snack mix.

Chaat masala is a tangy Indian spice blend, made with amchur – green mango powder. It's widely available in Indian supermarkets and a jar of the spice is well worth having in your cupboard. If you want to make your own, toast 1 tbsp cumin seeds, 1 tsp coriander seeds and ½ tsp fennel seeds until they become aromatic. Add them into a spice grinder with 1½ tbsp amchur powder, 1 tsp black salt, ½ tsp ground ginger, ½ tsp ajwain seeds, a pinch of dried mint and a pinch of asafoetida powder and blend to a powder before adding to snacks.

- 1 tbsp ghee or coconut oil
- 60 g (2 oz) puffed water lily seeds (sold as *makhana, phool makhana* or fox nuts)
- ½ tsp toasted cumin seeds
- 1 tsp chaat masala spice blend (see recipe introduction)

Melt the ghee in a pan over a low heat, then add the lily seeds, stirring continuously so they don't burn. The seeds might shrink as they cook – after a few minutes of cooking, try a seed and if it's crunchy that means it's cooked. Add the spices and toss to coat the seeds.

Eat straight away or store in an airtight container in a cupboard and eat within a couple of weeks.

SERVES 4

Water Lily Seed Pudding

Makhana Kheer is a traditional Indian milk pudding often eaten on Hindu fasting days, and this recipe is based on that dish. The powdered seeds provide not only comforting nourishment, but also act as a thickener for the milky spiced pudding.

2 tsp ghee
50g (1½ cups) puffed water lily seeds (sold as *makhana, phool makhana* or fox nuts)
500 ml (17fl oz/2 cups) full-fat milk
seeds from 4 cardamom pods (or ½ tsp ground cardamom)
a few strands of saffron
3 tbsp granulated sugar

TO SERVE

80 g (3 oz/½ cup) nuts (mix of pistachios, flaked/slivered almonds and cashews)
handful of sultanas (golden raisins)

Heat the ghee in a frying pan (skillet) until hot, then add the lily seeds and fry until golden and crunchy (they will smell like popcorn when they are ready). Place two-thirds of the seeds in a food processor and blitz to a fine powder. Set aside along with the remaining lily seeds.

Heat the milk in a deep, heavy-based saucepan, stirring continuously to prevent it catching on the bottom of the pan. Bring to the boil, then immediately turn the heat as low as possible and stir in the powdered and whole lily seeds, cardamon, saffron and sugar. Cook for a further 10 minutes, or until the liquid has started to thicken (it will thicken more when it is off the heat).

Once thick, remove from the heat, pour into serving bowls and sprinkle with nuts and sultanas.

This can be served as a hot pudding or chilled (it will thicken even more in the refrigerator).

FLAVOUR PROFILE Floral · Perfumed · Bitter · Intense

Jasmine

COMMONLY USED EDIBLE SPECIES

Jasminum officinale (common jasmine), *Jasminum sambac* (Arabian jasmine), *Jasmine grandiflorum* (Spanish jasmine).

WHERE THEY GROW

Jasmine thrives in full sun to partial shade, in well-drained, fertile soil.

WHEN TO GATHER

Late spring until autumn (fall).

The very mention of jasmine flowers might conjure up thoughts of inhaling the heady perfume on sultry summer nights – perhaps your imagination might be taking you to somewhere far more exotic than your current surroundings – to historical Arabia perhaps? If it has, you've daydreamed yourself into one of the places most associated with the plant and its perfume, the location the scented flower is thought to have originated before it began its long journey across continents, enchanting everyone with its unmistakable aroma.

PARTS USED

① Flowers

CAUTION

Only a few jasmine species are edible; make sure you use an edible species.

Jasmine doesn't just transport people in daydreams, though, it also helps carry them into a restful sleep – its essential oil being one of the most widely used for aiding slumber. With properties that calm body and mind, relieve stress and anxiety, it's a beloved oil in aromatherapists' fragrant tool kits.

If you were in your daydream of a hot Arabian night, you'd probably enjoy jasmine for another of its sleep-aiding benefits: for cooling. Jasmine's ability to reduce temperatures isn't lost on those who live in warm climates – it has long been used in drinks, including soothing *sharbats* in India and *Nam Loy Dok Mali* (jasmine-scented sweet water) in Thailand – well worth making if your weather forecasts a humid night ahead. Simply collect your flowers in the morning, ideally when they are still in bud, soak them in water until the evening and your drink will be ready for bedtime – you'll be glad you did when you drift off into dreamland.

You might have already tasted jasmine in the form of a flavoured black or green tea. Jasmine is so potent that rather than drinking an infusion of the flowers, these teas are made by simply placing the blossoms in between layers of dried camellia tea leaves, pressed down with a weight and then left to infuse for a few days. The aromatic oils drawn into the dried leaves flavour them with their soothing, delicious scent.

Jasmine's concentrated perfume means that you're unlikely to eat mouthfuls of the flower directly – in fact, even chewing on a single flower would be a rather bitter affair (imagine spraying your favourite perfume straight into your mouth). Jasmine is best used to perfume food by being infused into a carrier of its flavour first – like the Thai infused water mentioned above, which is used splashed over fruits and in baking to flavour desserts. Where you find rare recipes that call for whole flowers (such as Yunnanese egg dishes, see page 170) they're often paired with other strong flavours – mint, chilli, coriander (cilantro) – ones that can hold their own alongside the plant's incredible perfume.

However you want to consume your jasmine, make sure to carefully pick the right edible species of the plant, as the jasmine scent you've probably been inhaling probably isn't from an edible jasmine. The flower known as night-scented jasmine, which fills the evening air with its intoxicating fragrance, is in fact a different species of plant altogether (*Cestrum nocturnum*). Although it smells delicious, like a number of jasmine-named plants, it is actually inedible. It may be an intoxicating smell but it's also sadly toxic eating. Use that flower to scent your evening air, and only eat or drink from the edible jasmines – that way lies fragrant, sweet dreams.

SERVES 4 AS A SIDE DISH

Jasmine Eggs with Mint and Coriander Salad

The Yunnan province sits in the furthest south-westerly corner of China, touching the Tropic of Cancer. Its warm climate allows flowering plants to grow profusely, and the food from this region naturally reflects this abundance, often including luscious herbs and edible flowers as mainstay ingredients. One of the most compelling plates visitors to the region discover is a simple egg omelette filled with jasmine flower buds.

This dish can be made with fresh buds, but is also lovely with soaked dried flowers if you don't have access to the flora of Yunnan in your own garden.

4 large eggs
10 g (½ oz) fresh or rehydrated jasmine flowers (rehydrated in a couple of changes of water to reduce bitterness in the flowers)
salt and white pepper, to taste
3 tbsp vegetable oil

FOR THE SALAD

2 tsp rice wine vinegar
1 tsp light soy sauce
1 tsp sesame oil
¼ tsp chilli oil (or 1 finely chopped deseeded red chilli)
1 scant tsp sugar
50 g (1¾ oz) coriander (cilantro)
25 g (1 oz) mint
1 red onion, finely sliced

For the salad, combine the vinegar, soy sauce, oils and sugar and pour over the mint, coriander and onion in a bowl. Leave to marinate while you make the omelette.

Whisk the eggs until smooth and light, then stir in the jasmine flowers and season with salt and white pepper.

Heat the oil in a wok or frying pan (skillet) until hot, then pour in the eggs, swirling the mixture around the pan so it spreads into an omelette shape. Cook for 1–2 minutes before flipping and frying on the other side until both sides are golden and the eggs are cooked through.

Cut the omelette into quarters and serve warm with the salad.

Jasmine *Sharbat*

Sharbats are drinks made with infusions of fruit, herbs and flowers, first drunk by the Mughals in sixteenth-century India to cool the heat and humidity of hot summer days. Jasmine *sharbats* not only have cooling properties but are also thought to help regulate the immune system, boost mood and reduce insomnia – the perfect drink to serve to hot and bothered loved ones.

MAKES 1 × 250 ML (8½ FL OZ/1 CUP) BOTTLE

200 g (7 oz/scant 1 cup) granulated sugar
6 cardamom pods, crushed in a pestle and mortar
pinch of saffron
½ cup of fresh jasmine flowers

Put 175 ml (6 fl oz/¾ cup) water and sugar in a pan and heat until the sugar has dissolved. Turn the heat off as soon as the syrup is clear and leave to cool slightly until warm. Stir in the cardamom and saffron, then add the jasmine flowers, cover and leave to infuse overnight.

Strain and decant the syrup into a sterilised bottle and store in the refrigerator, where it will keep for a few weeks. Serve by diluting in water or chilled milk with lots of ice.

Jasmine and Fennel Poached Chicken Breasts

Jasmine flowers pair beautifully with chicken, poaching the breasts in a liquor infused with the flowers along with aromatic fennel adds a delicate flavour to the meat. The cooking liquid can also be used as a light soup or broth for a bowl of noodles or rice.

SERVES 4

4 tsp fresh jasmine flowers (2 tsp dried flowers)
4 skinless chicken breasts
½ fennel bulb, finely sliced
2 celery sticks, finely sliced
2 carrots, finely sliced
2 garlic cloves, finely chopped
1 small bunch each of tarragon and parsley, chopped
2 glasses of white wine
salt and black pepper, to taste

Place the jasmine flowers in a saucepan and cover with 2 litre (68 fl oz/8 cups) water. Bring to a simmer, then turn off the heat and leave to infuse for 10 minutes before removing the flowers with a slotted spoon.

Add the chicken breasts to the jasmine stock, then add all the vegetables and herbs along with the wine. Season with salt and pepper and poach over a low heat for 10 minutes, or until the chicken breasts are cooked through (push a sharp knife into the thickest part of the meat; if the juices run clear, the chicken is cooked).

You can serve the chicken in the vegetable broth or remove it from the liquid and serve with a salad.

Jasmine and Coconut Rice Pudding

You'd be forgiven for thinking that jasmine rice was flavoured with jasmine flowers, but it isn't. Not only is it not flavoured with jasmine, it doesn't taste like it either – the name is purely due to the rice grains' creamy, jasmine-like colour. It does go very well with jasmine, however, especially in creamy rice puddings. If so inclined, you could make this rice pudding with jasmine rice. It is also delicious served with slices of griddled pineapple. If you don't have jasmine rice to hand but do have a packet of short-grain pudding rice, be assured, it'll still make a delicious pudding.

SERVES 2

400 ml (14 fl oz/generous 1½ cups) coconut milk
10 g (½ oz/1 cup) of fresh jasmine flowers (or 1 tbsp dried jasmine flower buds)
50 g (1¾ oz/¼ cup) pudding rice (or short-grain pudding rice)
2 tbsp caster (superfine) sugar

Pour the coconut milk and any solids from the tin into a saucepan and heat, whisking, until the liquid starts to steam. Add two-thirds of the flowers to the pan and leave to infuse over a low heat for 20 minutes before removing with a slotted spoon. Add the rice and sugar to the perfumed milk and cook, stirring frequently until the rice has swollen and softened (if the rice starts to dry out, add a splash of water).

Serve hot or chilled, scattered with the remaining flowers. (If you used dried flowers, crumble the flowers up onto the pudding.)

Jasmine Tea, Lychee and Mango Jellies

Jasmine and lychees feature together in now cult-like *boba* or bubble teas. This dessert is a more refined, but equally refreshing affair, perfect for cleansing jaded palates at the end of a meal.

SERVES 4

400 ml (14 fl oz/generous 1½ cups) just-boiled water
2 tsp dried jasmine flowers or 2 jasmine tea bags
4 sheets of leaf gelatine
4 tbsp sugar, to taste
½ firm mango, peeled and cubed
10 lychees, peeled
single (light) cream, to serve (optional)

Make the jasmine tea by pouring 400 ml (14 fl oz/generous 1½ cups) just-boiled water over the flowers and leave to infuse for 10 minutes before straining.

Soak the gelatine leaves in a bowl of cold water until they become swollen and floppy. Remove the gelatine from the bowl and place into a bowl of 300 ml (10 fl oz/1¼ cups) of hot (but not boiling) water, stirring until the gelatine is dissolved. Add the jasmine tea, followed by the sugar, a teaspoonful at a time, testing for sweetness before you add any more. Pour the liquid into a small plastic container and refrigerate for about 4 hours to set.

When set, tip the jelly out from the container onto a chopping board and cut it into small cubes. Place in individual bowls with the cubed mango and lychees and serve as a refreshing pudding, or even as a breakfast, with or without a drizzle of cream.

FLAVOUR PROFILE

Fig leaves taste of coconut, vanilla, and almond with a hint of green herbal flavour. The coconut and vanilla flavour intensifies when the leaves are dried, especially if heated. Unripe figs have a similar flavour to the leaves; with a distinctive fig fruit flavour.

Fig

COMMONLY USED EDIBLE SPECIES

Ficus carica (var. Brown Turkey) are the most commonly grown for food.

WHERE THEY GROW

Figs grow best in warm, sheltered sites, such as against a wall where they benefit from the warmth in the stone. They fruit best when their roots are constrained by planting in a pot or by placing slabs into the ground around the tree.

WHEN TO GATHER

Leaves and latex sap — spring–late autumn (fall)

Fruit — summer and autumn

You may be wondering why fig trees are included in a book about edible flowering plants, given that if you've ever seen anything resembling a flower on a fig you've probably been looking at the wrong tree. But they do have flowers, hundreds of thousands of them just hidden from view, because inside each plump, jammy fig is a garden of tiny flowers. When you bite into a fig you can see the thin flowering stems and feel the crunch of the seeds that grew on the individual flowers. There's no doubt figs have or are, in fact, flowers.

PARTS USED

① Fruit (ripe and green)
② Leaves
③ Latex sap

Fruit or flower, they captured the hearts and taste buds of people a long time ago, which led them to be amongst the first fruits cultivated for eating. It was a fig tree that Buddha chose to sit under leading up to his famous moment of enlightenment. The Buddha's fig was a species aptly known as the Sacred Fig – a tender species that only thrives in the warmest of climates. Fortunately, the fig we mostly eat, *carica*, is a tougher tree, and will produce lots of lush leafy growth far further from the equator than where the Buddha sat.

Just as sacred figs need warmth to thrive, the fig tree in your garden needs hot summers to ripen any of its fruits (or should we say flowers?) and you might find your tree is only ever covered in tiny, green, bullet-hard figs. But don't despair if your tree doesn't hang heavy with ripe fruit – you still have harvests to enjoy, and they come not only from the unripe figs themselves but also the leaves and the white latex sap that drips out of the plant.

First, to your most abundant harvest: the leaves. Fig leaves are crammed full of the most incredible flavours – a cross between coconut, vanilla, almond and, of course, fig – all faintly present in a fresh leaf but released when the leaves are heated or dried, like a sweet-smelling air freshener. Infusing a fresh handful into warm syrup, cream or alcohol will pull out their green aromatic flavours into your food. Toasting the leaves before you infuse them not only makes the flavours stronger but means you can store them until you crave the warming scent that figs provide (mid-winter puddings, custards and liqueurs are far more comforting with fig-leaf flavour). You can store your dried fig leaves either whole or ground into a powder (if you find the stems don't break down, rub the powdered leaves through a sieve and you'll have a dust fine enough to scatter into baking). The leaves aren't only used to infuse flavour, you can eat them just like vine leaves; in fact, the oldest ancient Greek recipe recorded for stuffing leaves calls for fig rather than vine leaves, which were made into *dolmas* and cooked in a bath of honey to create little treats known called *thrions*.

Fig leaves aren't only destined for sweet baking; in fact, they're widely used as a savoury food – even being used as a vegetable in kitchens of places such as the Chinese province of Yunnan, where the opening buds and young leaves are fried in pakora-style batters, or cooked in a sour vinegar-based sauce, flavoured with chilli and garlic. Elsewhere, fig leaves are eaten in fragrant Thai-inspired curries, vegetable soups or used as the most incredible aromatic wrappers for fish.

If you are lucky enough to have an abundant harvest of ripe figs, head to Africa and the Mediterranean for inspiration on how to use the jammy fruit. In Algeria, figs lace lamb tagines and are used to fill sweet treats known as *makroud*. In Kenya, they are roasted before being drizzled in honey and a sprinkle of salt. People across the Mediterranean also make good use of unripe figs, turning them into chutneys, jams and preserves (like Greek *syko gilko* where they are preserved like candies in syrup, with almonds and other flavourings inserted into the little green fruits as a 'sweet spoon', served to visitors in Greek homes as a traditional gesture of hospitality).

Finally, there is the white latex from the tree, a thick, pure white, sticky substance that appears at a break (you will see this if you break a leaf stem or fruit from the tree). Full of acids, the milky liquid has a long history of being used to curdle milk to make cheese – it even got a mention in Homer's *The Iliad*, where he wrote about making cheese with the milky sap. (If you want to try your hand at cheesemaking, make sure you wash any sap from your skin, as the acids in the sap can irritate the skin, especially in sunlight.)

Although you may not find the nirvana of ripe fruit on your fig tree, once you discover your own enlightenment, that the leaves, unripe fruit and sap provide incredible flavours, textures and almost magical cheesemaking abilities, you'll be liberated from the fetters of craving just the sweet fruit. The Buddha would be proud of you. No wonder he chose the fig tree to sit under.

MAKES 500 G (1 LB 2 OZ)

Fig Curd Cheese

Fig twigs, leaves and fruit all contain an enzyme called ficin, which has been used as a vegetarian rennet for thousands of years. Rennets do the all-important role of splitting milk into curds and whey – a vital process in cheesemaking. Fig sap can be used to make all manner of cheeses, from soft curd cheese eaten within a few days to hard cheeses that are traditionally wrapped in fig leaves to absorb the sweet scent as the cheese matures. Traditionally, sheep's or goat's milk is used with fig rennet; if you use cow's milk, use less of the sap as it can cause cow's milk to turn bitter. (This cheese is a soft curd cheese, ideally eaten within a few days.)

2 litres (70 fl oz/8 cups) full-fat raw or unhomogenised milk, ideally sheep's or goat's milk
1 tsp natural live yoghurt
10 drops of fig sap (from the end of a fruit or leaf stem), diluted in 2 tbsp milk
2 fig leaves
salt, to taste (optional)

You will need a food thermometer

Pour the milk into a spotlessly clean pan (not aluminium or cast iron) and gently warm it to 38°C (100°F). Remove from the heat and stir in the live yoghurt. Leave for 15 minutes, keeping it at the same temperature, before gently stirring in the fig sap diluted in milk. Cover with a clean cloth and leave to sit for anything from 30 minutes to overnight until the curds have split from the whey.

Slice the curds (the solids) with a knife as if you were cutting the shape of a chess board (this will help release more whey). Use a slotted spoon to scoop the curds into a sieve (strainer) lined with muslin (cheesecloth) with a couple of fig leaves in the bottom. Let any whey drain from the curds, then tie the cheesecloth with string and hang the cheese up to drip for a few hours (over the sink is ideal).

Once the cheese has stopped dripping, untie the cloth and spoon the cheese into a bowl. Add salt to taste, if required. Cover and store in the refrigerator until needed. The cheese will become sourer over time and is best used within a couple of days.

MAKES
4 X 250 G
(9 OZ) JARS

Unripe Fig Jam

Unripe figs are an almost universal problem for fig-tree owners, and almost universally the solution to an unripe fig is to turn it into something sweet and covered in syrup – unripe fig jam. Some cultures flavour their green fig jams with cinnamon, others by stuffing them with nuts. This version of the preserve adds more flavour with dried fig leaves, making an already delicious preserve and syrup something to write home about (wherever in the universe you and your fig tree live).

- about 30 hard green figs or enough to fill a 1 litre (34 fl oz/4 cups) container
- 1 kg (2 lb 4 oz/4½ cups) granulated sugar
- zest of 1 unwaxed organic lemon
- 2 dried fig leaves

Wash your figs, trimming off any woody stalks. Cut a cross into the stalk end of each fig and use a needle to prick holes all around each fig (you might find that white sap oozes from the holes – this is a bitter latex that can be removed by soaking in water; wash your hands if you get the sap on your skin as it can irritate if left on). Place the figs in a large bowl, cover with water and leave to soak overnight.

The next day, drain the figs. If you find they are sticky with the sap, scrub them with warm water and a vegetable scrubber. Place the cleaned figs in a fresh pan of water, bring to the boil and simmer for a few minutes until they start to feel tender to the touch. Drain and set aside.

Heat the sugar in a pan with 1 litre (34 fl oz/4 cups) water until the sugar is dissolved and the syrup is clear. Add the lemon zest and dried fig leaves, carefully place the figs into the syrup and bring to the boil, then immediately turn down to a gentle simmer and cook for 30 minutes. Turn off the heat and leave overnight to soak.

The next day, bring the pan to a gentle simmer for another 30 minutes. Test by removing a fig from the pan and slicing it in half – if the fig looks almost translucent all the way through and is tender, they are ready. Spoon the figs into sterilised jars, cover with the piping hot syrup and seal (turn upside down to help sterilise the lid). If you want to keep the figs for more than a few weeks, pasteurise them in a water bath.

MAKES A 20 CM (8 IN) CAKE

Pan Di Higo – Dried Fig Cake

During the Roman Empire, and probably well before then, figs were preserved for eating through the winter and, as all good ancient people knew, the best way to preserve fruit was by drying it out and adding spices for good measure. Roman gastronomes pounded figs along with a liberal handful of sesame seeds and spices before wrapping the mixture in fig leaves and drying in the hot sun. Variations of this recipe can be found all across the Mediterranean today. Andalusian fig cake, or *pan di higo*, is made with very similar ingredients and is absolutely delicious served in slices with Manchego, chorizo and wine. The Romans would have approved.

If you want to dry your own figs for this recipe, you must pick figs that aren't too ripe, cut them in half, arrange them on a heatproof rack, and place them in a dehydrator or oven at 50°C (125°F/gas ¼) for around 10 hours. If you happen to live in a hot climate, you can dry your figs in the sun over a few days; just remember to bring the figs inside at night so they don't rehydrate in the dew.

- 350 g (12 oz) dried figs
- 100 ml (3½ fl oz/scant ½ cup) sherry
- 50 g (1¾ oz/⅓ cup) blanched almonds
- 50 g (1¾ oz/⅓ cup) blanched hazelnuts
- 30 g (1 oz/3 tbsp) sesame seeds
- small pinch of ground cloves
- 10 g (½ oz/2 tbsp) ground cinnamon
- 4 tsp honey
- 10 fig leaves

Soak the dried figs overnight in the sherry.

The next day, preheat the oven to 135°C (275°F/gas 1).

Place the almonds and hazelnuts in a heavy frying pan (skillet) and toast for a few minutes, adding the sesame seeds as the nuts start to colour. Place the nuts and seeds in a food processor and pulse a couple of times to start to break them up. Pour the nuts and seeds into a mixing bowl.

Chop the soaked figs into small pieces, then place in the processor and blitz to a paste. Add the fig paste to the mixing bowl with the nuts and seeds, then add the cloves, cinnamon and honey, and stir to incorporate, adding more sherry if the mixture is crumbly.

Line a 20 cm (8 in) cake tin (pan) with the fig leaves, making sure they are overlapping each other and reach up the sides of the pan. Spoon the fig mixture into the pan and fold over the fig leaves to cover the top (add more leaves on the top if there are any gaps). Press down with a weighted flat plate. Bake in the oven for 30 minutes, then remove and let the cake cool down in the pan.

Once cool, turn the cake out onto a plate and leave in a ventilated area to help dry out before wrapping in parchment and storing in an airtight container for up to 3 months.

SERVES 4

Fig and Halloumi Baked in a Fig Leaf with Walnuts

Before we put on our winter thermals, there may be a few sunny days left to enjoy where we can pretend it is still summer. There are few better ways to tie up the loose ends of summer than with the last of the figs and first of the year's walnuts, cooked with halloumi and served with honey and a drizzle of sweetly sharp balsamic. Using fig leaves to bundle up the delicious trio not only looks beautiful but also permeates the parcel with the warming, almost nutmeg scent of fig leaves – a nod to the warming spices of winter to come.

8 large figs
16 medium or 8 large fresh fig leaves
100 g (3½ oz) halloumi, cut into 8 rectangles
50 g (1¾ oz) walnuts (fresh if you can get them)
1 tbsp runny honey
olive oil, for drizzling
balsamic vinegar, for drizzling

Preheat the oven to 180°C (350°F/gas 4).

Place each fig in the centre of a fig leaf (if you are using smaller leaves, use two leaves per bundle, laying one on top of the other in a star shape). Score a cross into the top of each fig and stuff with a piece of halloumi cheese and a few of the walnuts. Wrap the leaves around the fig and tie them up with butcher's string or twine to form a bundle.

Place the parcels on a baking sheet and bake for 15 minutes, or until the halloumi is melted and the fig softened.

Open the parcels and drizzle over the honey, a little olive oil and balsamic vinegar. Serve with cured meats or bread.

SERVES 2

Sea Bass Cooked in Fig Leaves with Oregano and Lemons

Wrapping fish in fig leaves is a Greek tradition dating back to 400 BC. We know this fact thanks to the poet Archestratus who, as well as being clever with words, was also rather adept in culinary matters, and is regarded as the father of gastronomy, writing the world's first known cookbook. One of the recipes he recorded was for fish cooked in fig leaves, with marjoram – and should you wrap your fish in fig leaves with marjarom you'll realise why he is so highly regarded.

This dish is ideally cooked in the heat of the Mediterranean sun on embers, but is also very lovely on a grill on a drizzly autumnal evening.

2 small or 1 large sea bass (gutted)
6 large fig leaves
4 tsp marjoram or 2 tsp oregano leaves
1 lemon, thinly sliced
salt, to taste

First, cut five lengths of butcher's twine that are long enough to tie around the fish and lay them on a board a few centimetres (1 in) apart. Place the fig leaves on top of the twine, making sure that all the leaves overlap.

Prepare the fish by removing any loose scales by scraping a blunt knife along the fish from the tail to the head. Wash the fish and pat it dry with a kitchen towel (including inside its cavity).

Open the cavity up and sprinkle with most of the marjoram and a pinch of salt, along with a couple of slices of lemon and half a piece of fig leaf. Close the cavity and lay the fish onto the fig leaves. Place the remaining lemon on top of the fish. Drizzle with olive oil and the remaining marjoram. Fold the fig leaves around the fish, wrapping it in a parcel – make sure to completely wrap the fish, including its head and tail. Secure the parcel by tying the lengths of twine.

Place the fish on a barbecue or a griddle on a hob and cook over a gentle heat. Place a lid over the fish whilst it cooks – cook on each side for at least 5 minutes – the leaves will become charred and will infuse the fish with their nutty, smoky flavour.

Remove the fish from the barbecue or griddle and unwrap – serve with potatoes and a green salad.

SERVES 4

Fig Leaf and Roasted Plums with Marsala Syrup

The best kind of cooking is not only easy, but gives you far more than you put in – this is one of those best kinds of recipes, a few halved plums, some leaves, a sprinkle of sugar and a splash of fortifed wine not only creates the most delicious sticky roast plums that taste like figs, but you're also left with a gift – sticky plummy fig leaves that you can soak in marsala to make a very easy, very satifiying tipple; so good it's probably worth increasing the quanities you make this pudding in.

12 firm plums
4 large fig leaves
3 tbsp unrefined sugar
500 ml (17 fl oz/generous 2 cups) Marsala or sherry
4 ginger snap biscuits
150 ml (5 fl oz/scant ⅔ cup) custard or thick cream

Preheat the oven to 160°C (350°F).

Slice your plums in half and remove the stones.

Place two fig leaves on the base of a lidded baking dish, scatter with the sugar and pour over 3 tbsp of water before placing the plums facing down onto the sugared leaves. Top with the remaining leaves, cover with a well-fitting lid and place in the oven. Cook for 20 minutes, remove both the lid and the top leaves (do not discard them) and turn the plums over so that they are facing upwards, turn the oven down to 120°C (275°F) and cook without a lid for for another 10 minutes.

When the plums have become sticky, remove them from the pan and place in indiviual pudding bowls. Place the pan back on the heat and deglaze the sticky syrup with enough of the Marsala to create a pourable syrup. Place the sticky fig leaves into a jar and cover with the remaining Marsala for a day or so – their flavours will infuse, creating a delicious figgy, plummy liqueur.

To serve the plums, crumble a ginger biscuit over them, add a good dollop of cream or custard and drizzle over the plum and fig marsala syrup. Crumble up the dried fig leaf that had been on top of the cooking plums, and scatter flecks of the leaf over the syrup.

FLAVOUR PROFILE Bitter · Spiced · Peppery · Earthy · Some varieties fruity with citrus flavours

Marigold

COMMONLY USED EDIBLE SPECIES

Calendula officinalis (pot marigold), *Calendula arvensis* (field marigold), *Tagetes erecta* (Mexican marigold), *Tagetes patula* (French marigold), *Tagetes filifolia* (Irish lace marigold), *Tagetes lucida* (Mexian mint/tarragon), *Tagetes tenuifolia* (lemon marigold).

WHERE THEY GROW

Tagetes species like fertile, slightly acidic or neutral soil and they benefit from full sun.

Calendula species thrive in rich soil that retains moisture, preferring cooler climates compared to Tagetes.

WHEN TO GATHER

Late spring–late autumn

When you read the word marigold your mind's eye may be visualising a flower that looks like an orange daisy, with oval, scented leaves and curled seed heads, or you could well be thinking of a more frilly flower head, growing from plants that have serrated leaves. These two plants are both marigolds and both part of the daisy (*Asteraceae*) family, both revered and symbolic, but they're actually quite different plants. The daisy-like flower is a *Calendula*, the frillier flower is a *Tagetes* – if you always thought the two were both types of the same species and are questioning your botanical understanding, you are not alone – the confusion about the two marigolds started hundreds of years ago, long before we planted them in our modern-day gardens.

PARTS USED

① Flowers of *Calendula* and *Tagetes*.

② Leaves and stems of *Calendula* and some *Tagetes*, including *T. tenuifolia* and *T. patula* (check your species for edibility of the leaves).

CAUTION

Avoid large amounts of *Calendula* and *Tagetes* if you are pregnant or breastfeeding. Not all species of *Tagetes* are edible – make sure you select edible forms of the plant (see above).

Tagetes and *Calendula* started their lives in different parts of the world, both radiating their bright yellow flowers in their own lands. *Calendula* has had an ancient and illustrious career as a revered flower. In India, China and Europe it has a long association with the main religions that spread across each continent; seen as connecting people with the heavenly realms, images of the flowers adorn ancient texts, buildings and clothing. In warmer climates, you might find *Calendula* flowering all year round – its ability to bloom throughout the year earning it its name, from the Latin *calendae*, or little calendar. Its other name, pot marigold, was given for two reasons. Firstly, legend holds that the Virgin Mary used flowers instead of coins; as a result, offerings of marigold (*Calendula*) flowers are left at her altars (far cheaper than leaving the gold coins that the church might well have preferred). Secondly, the 'pot' part refers to the way it was used as a cooking herb. It was utilised across Europe for everything from flavouring wines to colouring cheeses and puddings. In Germany, its flowers and leaves were added to soups and stews.

At the same time, *Tagetes* were equally idolised in their homelands of South America, where they were used in the most revered of celebrations: *Dia de los Muertos* – the Day of the Dead (another symbol of connection to the afterlife). Used to line pathways to graves, the flower was also turned into drinks and eaten as a symbolic food. Known as *cempasuchil* (meaning 20-petalled flower) the flowers were, and still are, pressed into tortillas, stirred through savoury dishes of onions and rice, cooked into a sauce with almonds to serve with chicken, and infused into custard tarts. *Dia de los Muertos* remains a marigold-flavoured feast.

Quite how *Tagetes* arrived in Eurasia is less down to heavenly intervention and more down to a drive to colonise. When the Spanish and Portuguese colonised South America, they brought the plant back across the Atlantic where it travelled with the warm trade winds to India. Some claim that the Christian sailors on board called the plant marigold – perhaps it was the sailors who were the cause of hundreds of years of confusion? Whether they were at fault or not, they introduced the flower to the Indian subcontinent, where the warmth-loving plant thrived, and pushed the more demure *Calendula* into the background, replacing it as the flower of choice to decorate weddings, festivals and even funerals. As a result, it took not only *Calendula*'s common name but also its position in society. The new arrival soon trailed its way across the silk roads and spice routes, decorating lands and festivals as it travelled. Today, from India to the Caucasus, huge fields of *Tagetes* marigolds are grown to assuage the hunger for the plant.

Fortunately for gardeners, marigolds don't only share names and ceremonial symbolism, but also their use in the garden and kitchen. Both *Calendula* and *Tagetes* share the same strong aromas that are a deterrent to pests but deliciously interchangeable in recipes. Marigold, Mary's gold, *Tagetes* or *Calendula* all make food and drinks taste heavenly, no matter which plant you choose to use.

SERVES 4

Bazhe Sauce

Squeezed between the borders of Eastern Europe, the Middle East and Western Asia lies Georgia. Sitting in the path of armies, traders and travellers who wove their influences into its culture and cuisine, it would have been easy for Georgia to have become just an amalgamation of others' traditions, yet somehow, perhaps like a squeezed-in-the-middle sibling, Georgia has managed to pluck the most delicious offerings from their neighbours' overhanging trees whilst holding onto the unique flavours that make Georgia Georgia. And one of those things comes from *Tagetes* marigolds and blue fenugreek, which Georgian cuisine proudly holds as its own, used to flavour *bazhe* sauce, a delicious blend of spices, nuts and garlic – a condiment as proudly Georgian as its people.

Bazhe sauce is delicious served with a simply roasted chicken and green beans; or made into *nigvziani badrijani*, a rolled aubergine (eggplant) starter made by spreading a layer of the sauce over cooled, pan-fried slices of aubergine, before rolling the slices like stubby cigars and garnishing them with coriander (cilantro), basil, pomegranate seeds and a few marigold petals. *Calendula* marigold flowers can be used in place of *Tagetes* in this recipe.

- 200 g (7 oz) shelled walnuts (taste them first to ensure they're not bitter)
- 2 garlic cloves
- ½ tsp ground blue fenugreek (available from online spice shops)
- ½ tsp ground coriander
- ½ tsp paprika
- 2 heaped tsp or small handful of dried *Tagetes* marigold flowers, plus extra to serve
- 1 tsp white wine vinegar
- salt, to taste
- walnut oil, to serve (optional)

Place all of the ingredients apart from the salt in a food processor, add a splash of water and blend to a thick paste. Keep adding trickles of water until the paste has become a pourable, thick sauce. Season with white wine vinegar and salt, to taste.

To serve, drizzle with walnut oil and sprinkle over dried marigold flowers.

This sauce will keep for a few days in the refrigerator or can be frozen. If you don't use it straight away it will thicken, so loosen it with more water or a drizzle of walnut oil.

SERVES 4

Fried Potatoes with Svaneti Salt

Svaneti salt is a unique seasoning from the mountainous region of Georgia. Made with a blend of herbs, spices, salt and flowers, it is used both as a seasoning for dishes like these fried potatoes, but is also lovely used to flavour meats, tomatoes and even sliced cucumbers. The recipe will give you enough salt to fill a jar to use on other dishes.

FOR THE SVANETI SALT

10 g (½ oz) coriander seeds
10 g (½ oz) dill seeds
10 g (½ oz) blue fenugreek leaves (available from online spice shops)
10 g (½ oz) cumin seeds
5 g (¼ oz) paprika
10 g (½ oz) dried marigold flowers
2 garlic cloves, crushed
10 g (½ oz) sea salt flakes

FOR THE POTATOES

1 kg (2 lb 4 oz) potatoes, peeled and cut into 2 cm (¾ in) dice
8 tbsp light olive oil

TO SERVE

1 bunch of basil (purple basil if you have it), finely chopped
1 bunch of fresh parsley, finely chopped
handful of fresh marigold petals (use dried if you don't have fresh)

For the Svaneti salt, place the spices and marigold petals into a spice grinder and grind to a powder. Place the garlic and salt in a pestle and mortar and pound until you have a smooth paste. Place all of the ingredients into a bowl and thoroughly mix them together until they are all thoroughly incorporated. Spoon the damp mixture into a jar, and store for up to 12 months.

Place the potatoes in a pan of salted cold water, bring to the boil and cook for around 10 minutes, or until the potatoes are starting to cook but aren't soft. Drain and leave to dry in the colander for 1 hour.

Heat the oil in a large frying pan (skillet). Once the oil is very hot, add the potatoes and fry until golden and crisp. Sprinkle a teaspoon of the Svaneti salt over the potatoes, mix thoroughly and taste, adding more salt according to your preference.

Spoon the potatoes into a serving dish, sprinkle with the basil, parsley and fresh marigold petals and serve.

SERVES 4

Marigold and Courgette Risotto

Calendula marigolds and courgettes (zucchini) make delicious light, summer risottos. The *Calendula* flowers and leaves are both infused into the stock and a pesto-like seasoning oil that is equally beautiful used brushed on griddled courgettes as part of a summer salad. Should you have any oil leftover, it will keep in the refrigerator for up to two weeks. (If you use a *Tagetes* marigold in this recipe, choose a variety that has flavoursome leaves, and use young leaves, which tend to be less bitter.)

FOR THE OIL

- 6 *Calendula* marigold flower stems (including leaves)
- 3 tbsp extra virgin olive oil
- ¼ tsp finely grated lemon zest
- pinch of salt
- lemon juice, to taste

FOR THE RISOTTO

- 1 litre (34 fl oz/4¼ cups) vegetable or chicken stock
- 4 *Calendula* marigold flower stems, plus 4 flower heads to garnish
- 50 g (1¾ oz) butter
- 2 tbsp olive oil
- 2 shallots, finely diced
- 1 garlic clove, finely diced
- 350 g (12 oz/1½ cups) risotto rice
- 200 ml (7 fl oz/scant 1 cup) white wine
- 1 courgette (zucchini)

Wash and roughly chop the marigold flower stems and leaves, discarding any stems that are woody. Place in a mini blender with the olive oil, lemon zest and a good pinch of salt. Blend until smooth, and squeeze in enough lemon juice to suit your taste. Before you add the lemon juice, the oil will be quite bitter (like a strong olive oil); the more juice you add, the less bitter your oil will be. Once seasoned to taste, set aside while you make the risotto.

Heat the vegetable or chicken stock in a pan, then add the flower stems and leave to infuse for 10 minutes before straining.

Heat the butter and olive oil in a sauté pan over a medium heat, then add the shallots and garlic, and gently sweat until soft. Add the rice, stir to coat in the oniony butter and gently cook until the rice becomes semi-translucent. Pour in the white wine and stir with a wooden spoon to deglaze the pan, making sure nothing is sticking to the bottom. Once the rice has absorbed the wine, add a ladle of infused stock, stir and once the stock is absorbed add more. Repeat until all the stock has all been added, stirring continuously while the risotto cooks. Once the rice is al dente, vigorously stir to make it creamy, then remove from the heat and cover with a lid to rest (add more water if your risotto is too dry).

Meanwhile, peel and finely dice the courgette, and pull the petals from the last 4 *Calendula* flowers.

Spoon the risotto onto plates, scatter over the diced courgette, drizzle with the infused *Calendula* oil and sprinkle over the *Calendula* petals. Serve immediately.

SERVES 2

Marigold and Cinnamon Milk

Powdered marigold flowers are lovely infused into custard tarts and warm milky drinks. A teaspoonful added to golden, turmeric-flavoured milk adds both flavour and marigold's herbal benefits. A hot milk drink blending *Tagetes* marigold flowers with cinnamon and orange is drunk in Mexico during Day of The Dead celebrations. Known as *cempasúchil atole*, the drink is thickened with *masa*, a dough made from maize. If you want a thicker drink, you can add a slurry of cornflour to the milk and heat through until thickened.

To make the bright orange marigold powder, pull the petals from the flower head, dry and grind in a spice or coffee grinder. Both *Calendula* and *Tagetes* marigold flowers are delicious in this drink.

- 1 tsp powdered marigold flowers
- 500 ml (17 fl oz/generous 2 cups) whole milk
- 1 tbsp light brown sugar
- 1 cinnamon stick
- pared zest of ¼ orange

Place all of the ingredients into a pan and bring to a gentle simmer, stirring the milk frequently to make sure it doesn't catch on the bottom of the pan. Infuse the flowers and spices for 10 minutes before straining the milk.

Serve alone as a comforting drink or with a measure or two of rum for more of a kick.

MAKES 2

Calendula Martini

Herbalists' shelves bow under the weight of bottles of tinctures – herbs and flowers infusing in alcohol. Often among their tinctures will invariably be one made with *Calendula* flowers, used to soothe inflammation and pains. Tinctures are also at home on the shelves of cocktail cabinets, often in the form of bitters. A drop of the medicinal liquid finishes a cocktail, balancing bitter with sweet, sour and salt.

Orange peel and *Calendula* flowers and stems are beautiful together and turn the medicinal floral tincture into a bitters that elevates a martini to new herbal heights. To make orange and *Calendula* bitters, pack a little jam jar with sticky *Calendula* stems and flowers with a couple of twists of orange zest and cover with vodka. Leave for a couple of weeks before straining and bottling, ideally in a bottle with a pipette to dispense drops of your bitters into cocktails.

FOR THE VODKA

- 2 tbsp dried *Calendula* marigold flowers
- zest of 1 orange
- 300ml (10 fl oz/1¼ cups) good-quality vodka

FOR THE MARTINI

- 60 ml (4 tbsp) orange-and-calendula-infused vodka (see above)
- 20 ml (4 tsp) dry vermouth
- 10 ml (2 tsp) triple sec
- 2 dashes of orange and calendula bitters (see recipe introduction)
- *Calendula* flowers and orange zest, to garnish

To make an orange-and-calendula-infused vodka, place the orange zest and dried calendula flowers in a 330ml (11¼ fl oz/ 1¼ cup) jar, then pour over the vodka. Leave to infuse for 24 hours before tasting and straining the vodka (you can add a tablespoon of sugar to sweeten the vodka should you wish to drink it as a liqueur).

To make the cocktail, add the vodka, vermouth, triple sec and bitters to a cocktail shaker or tumbler filled with ice. Stir with a long spoon and strain into a chilled martini glass.

Serve with a *Calendula* flower and a twist of orange zest.

FLAVOUR PROFILE Tangy · Sour · Vinegary · Slight floral sweetness

Sumac

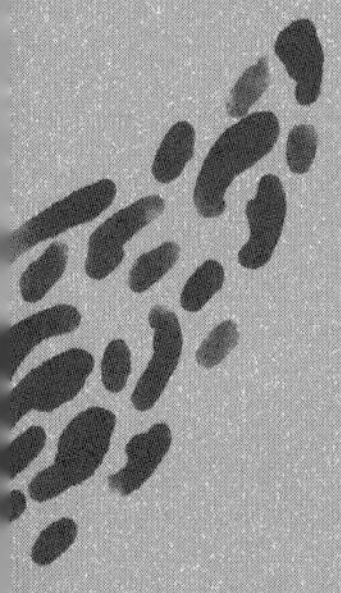

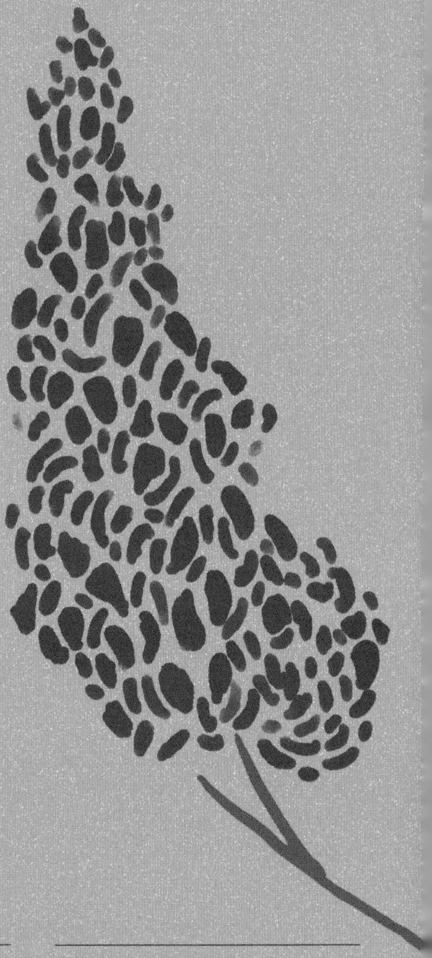

COMMONLY USED EDIBLE SPECIES

Edible varities most commonly used are *Rhus typhina* (staghorn sumac); *Rhus glabra* (smooth sumac); *Rhus coriaria* (Sicilian sumac).

WHERE THEY GROW

Sumac prefers fertile, moist, well-drained soil, ideally in full sun.

WHEN TO GATHER

Young tender shoots — spring and early summer

Berries (drupes) — late summer and early autumn (fall)

In the not too distant past jars of a red, sour powder started appearing in well-dressed Western spice racks, their contents dusted onto everything from hummus to meats, like the coating left behind after Saharan dust storms blow across continents. Cooks rejoiced – the search for tang was complete; a fruity tart alternative to lemons to sour and flavour food, which unlike citrus didn't rot in the fruit bowl, but could be kept all year in a jar. That powder was sumac, imported from the Mediterranean basin where it had been sprinkled onto and infused into food for thousands of years. The vibrant new arrival was a very welcome guest.

PARTS USED

① Berries
② Young shoots

CAUTION

All edible sumacs produce clusters of upright red berries. There are a few plants known as sumacs which are toxic – these include poison sumac, poison ivy and poison oak. Fortunately, none of these plants have red berries that look like edible sumac.

Also be aware that if you are allergic to cashews you can also have an allergic reaction to sumac.

But sumac is less of a newcomer than people may think, because no matter what continent you live in, you probably lived near sumac long before it appeared in jars in your spice cupboard. The type of sumac you may have encountered will depend on where you live, as climate and terrain all have a part to play in which varieties thrive. Across America you will find numerous types of sumac, from smooth sumac to rare fragrant sumac, and temperate-climate-loving staghorn sumac (it often appears in Northern Europe and Australasia as an introduced, vigorous spreading garden shrub).

It is now so widely planted in gardens that if you take a walk down your street you may well find a neighbour with a sumac plant – if they're the generous type, ask them in late summer if you could pluck a cluster of the red berries that perch at the end of the tree's branches. They may look at you with a perplexed expression, but take your cluster of berries home and give them a lick. Freshly ripened sumac is coated in tart acidity, so sour it'll make you wince (in a very delectable way). These sour berries are what is in the jars on supermarket shelves – gathered from trees that cover hillsides in the Middle East, dipped into a salt bath before being dried and ground into a fine powder. Your sumac is just that bit fresher and as a result crammed full of a sourer twang.

Used fresh from the tree, sumac can turn water into wine (quite literally as you can make wine with sumac), into a fruity, vibrant tea and perhaps most famously into sumacade – a Native American drink rich in vitamin C and antioxidants, made by simply plunging the clusters of berries on their stalk into a jug of water and leaving to infuse overnight. There's no lemonade that will beat sumacade as a sour thirst-quencher.

Back over in the Mediterranean basin, sumac berries are also infused in water, this time to make a sour liquid to use in cooking – just as you might use a splash of vinegar or a squeeze of citrus. The Romans used sumac to flavour vinegar in this way, making a condiment with a double hit of fruity sourness. If you happen to have a bottle of apple cider vinegar or white wine vinegar and a sumac drupe, you could do a lot worse than infusing the sumac into the vinegar to create a fruity, sour liquid that is even more delicious than the sum of its parts.

What makes sumac taste so sour? Its coating is high in malic acid – the same acid that makes apples sour and grapes sharp. But sumac also has an astringent, drying flavour – and this comes from tannins, which the whole plant is full of, so much so that sumacs were harvested for thousands of years to supply tannin to leather workers across the globe. In fact, the kind of sumac that is usually processed for consumption is *Rhus coriaria* (Sicilian sumac, otherwise known as Tanner's sumac), because it was regarded as the finest form of sumac for tanning – and eating. However, once you've eaten some fresh from your neighbour's tree, you'll know that the finest sumac for eating is the one growing in your street right now.

MAKES 1 200 ML (7 FL OZ/SCANT 1 CUP) JAR OF SUMAC SPICE

How to Process Sumac

Processing sumac to use later in the year can be as easy as drying the whole drupes and crumbling them with the seeds onto food. But, if you want a more refined texture without the crunch of the seeds, you'll need to remove the sour fluffy coating from the hard seeds. You'll end up with all the flavour but no crunch.

6 fresh sumac drupes (flower heads), collected after a sunny period
pinch of salt (optional)

Place the sumac flower heads into a dehydrator or very low oven (50°C/120°F) and dry for a few hours to remove excess moisture.

Pull the berries from the main stem. Place in a food processor and blitz with a plastic dough blade attachment until the red fluff lines the sides of the processor bowl and the hard seeds lie at the bottom. You can simply scoop out the fluffy spice from the bowl and discard the seeds.

Alternatively, place the fluff-covered sumac seeds in a coarse sieve or small-holed strainer and use the end of a wooden rolling pin to rub the sumac. The seeds will fall through the sieve and leave the light fluffy spice behind.

Lay the sumac out on a flat tray somewhere warm to thoroughly dry out before jarring. You can add a pinch of salt to the sumac (as is often done to sumac sold in shops) or store it by itself for up to 12 months.

SERVES 4

Roasted Sumac Carrots with Roasted Onion Yoghurt Sauce

Sweet roasted carrots are ideal bedfellows with whole sumac berries lying on a smoky yoghurt dip. If you have freshly harvested berries, so much the better, as the sweet carrots and yoghurt enhance the fruity sour flavour of the freshly ripened balls. This dish is lovely served with flatbreads for a light lunch or as part of a main meal.

1 kg (2 lb 4 oz) carrots, washed
olive oil, for drizzling
juice of 1 orange
the berries from 1 fresh sumac drupe, or 3 tsp dried sumac berries, or 2 tsp ground sumac
2 sweet onions, unpeeled and halved
200 g (7 oz/generous ¾ cup) Greek yoghurt
juice of ½ lemon
½ tsp smoked paprika
handful of parsley
handful of pomegranate seeds
salt, to taste

Preheat the oven to 230°C (450°F/gas 8).

If you have slender uniform carrots, simply slice them in half; if they are more of a wonky affair, chop them into rough carrot-shaped batons with a thicker end tapering into a slender tip. Place the carrots in a bowl and rub olive oil all over them and sprinkle with a pinch of salt. Place the carrots on a baking tray and squeeze over the orange juice. Sprinkle two thirds of the sumac berries (or powder) over the carrots.

Place the onion halves on a separate baking tray and drizzle with oil.

Roast in the oven for 35–45 minutes (turning the carrots over after 15 minutes), until the onions soften and the carrots are starting to caramelise.

Remove from the oven and let the onions cool slightly before pushing them out of their papery skins. Place the cooked onion onto a chopping board and finely chop to a mushy consistency. Scrape into a bowl and stir in the yoghurt, lemon juice, smoked paprika and a pinch of salt.

Place the carrots on a serving dish along with the onion yoghurt and sprinkle everything with the remaining sumac berries or powder, the parsley and a sprinkle of pomegranate seeds. Serve with flatbreads and salads.

SERVES 6

Lentil and Sumac Soup with Sumac and Coriander Butter

Sumac and lentils have a long history of being paired in sour, nourishing soups across the Middle East. This soup also pays homage to another sumac pairing – that of coriander. Sumac and coriander are delicious rubbed onto fish, meats and vegetables, and, as in this soup, used with pulses or grains. It's worth making at least a double batch of the butter to keep in the refrigerator (although if you want to store it for any length of time, it is best to use ghee in place of butter).

- 2 whole sumac drupes (or 2 tbsp ground sumac)
- 2 tsp olive oil
- 1 white onion, finely sliced
- 2 garlic cloves, minced
- 150 g (5½ oz/generous ¾ cup) green (Puy) lentils, washed and drained
- 1 litre (34 fl oz/4¼ cups) vegetable or chicken stock
- 200 g (7 oz) spinach
- 1 bunch of fresh coriander (cilantro), leaves and stems separated, stems finely chopped
- salt and black pepper, to taste

FOR THE SUMAC AND CORIANDER BUTTER

- 50 g (1¾ oz) butter or ghee
- 3 garlic cloves, smashed to a paste
- 1 tsp ground sumac, plus extra to serve
- ½ tsp ground coriander
- ½ tsp salt

Break the sumac flower heads up and crumble the berries into a small pan, cover with water and place over a gentle heat. Simmer for 5 minutes, then remove from the heat and leave for 30 minutes.

Strain the sumac mixture, discarding the berries and keeping the sumac-flavoured sour water.

Heat the oil in a large pan over a low heat, add the onion and garlic with a splash of water and a pinch of salt. Sweat until the onion is soft and starting to colour, then add the lentils and cook for a minute until the lentils have started to absorb the onion and garlic flavour. Pour in the stock and bring to the boil, removing any scum that may form on the top of the liquid. Once boiling, turn down to a low simmer and cook until the lentils are soft but not falling apart, for around 20–25 minutes.

Add the spinach and coriander stems, stir in the sumac-flavoured water and cook over a low heat until the spinach has wilted. Season with a pinch of salt (the butter sauce is salty so don't over-season the liquid.)

Meanwhile, make the butter sauce. Melt the butter or ghee in a pan with the garlic, ground sumac and coriander, and salt. When the garlic is turning a light golden colour, turn off the heat and set aside.

Spoon the soup into bowls, drizzle over the spiced butter and garnish with torn coriander leaves and a final sprinkle of ground sumac.

SERVES 4 AS A SIDE DISH

Onions with Sumac

Onions with sumac is something halfway between a salad and a pickle. A traditional Turkish dish called *sumaklı soğan salatası*, its sour, oniony zing adds a bright flavour to *meze*-style meals, or can be used as a pickle in pittas stuffed with kebab meats.

2 large onions, thinly sliced
½ tsp salt
1 tbsp lemon juice
1 tbsp ground sumac
½ tsp sugar (optional)
2 tbsp olive oil
small bunch of parsley, chopped

Soak the thinly sliced onions in water for 30 minutes, then drain and squeeze out any excess water.

Place the onions in a bowl, sprinkle over the salt, lemon juice and sumac, and massage into the onions. Taste for sourness – if the onions are too sour, add the sugar. Drizzle over the oil and stir in the parsley. Leave the mixture to mellow for at least 1 hour before serving.

This dish will keep for up to a week in a well-sealed jar.

MAKES
A 200 G
(7 OZ) JAR

Za'atar

The Levant is a region that has created some of the most delicious store cupboard ingredients of our globally inspired kitchen and za'atar is one of the most beloved – a perfect combination of nutty sesame, herbs, salt and sour sumac. Za'atar can be used for everything from flavouring meat, sprinkled onto hummus or labneh, or simply scattered onto olive-oil soaked breads. Whilst perfectly good jars of za'atar are available on supermarket shelves, as all the best Levantine cooks will tell you, nothing quite compares to the zing of freshly made za'atar.

2½ tbsp white sesame seeds
2 tbsp ground sumac (see p.205)
2 tbsp dried thyme
1 tbsp dried oregano
1 tbsp dried marjoram
½ tsp ground cumin
1 tsp sea salt

Heat a dry wok or large saucepan over a low heat. Pour in the sesame seeds, agitating the pan to keep the seeds moving until they start to toast. Scoop them out of the pan and add two-thirds of the seeds to a spice grinder along with the remaining ingredients. Grind until crumbly but not as fine as powder. Stir in the remaining sesame seeds and pour the blend into an airtight jar for up to 3 months to enjoy it at its freshest.

MAKES A 20 CM (8 IN) CAKE

Sumac and Orange Semolina Cake

Sumac may often find itself in savoury dishes, but it's just as useful and delicious as a sour ingredient in sweet food and drinks. Infusing the berries into sugar syrup makes a delicious syrup that can be used as a cordial, a cocktail ingredient or, perhaps in its finest hour, as a drizzle to pour over cakes, à la lemon drizzle cake. This semolina cake is soaked with sumac syrup. It's an unapologetically sweet cake, best served like baklava in little mouthful pieces. (And if you were wondering whether sumac syrup could be used in baklava-style pastries, you'd be absolutely right.)

FOR THE SYRUP

- 3 sumac flower drupes
- 300 ml (10 fl oz/1¼ cups) boiling water
- 250 g (9 oz/generous 1 cup) granulated sugar
- juice of 1 orange

FOR THE CAKE

- 250 g (9 oz) butter
- 220 g (8 oz/1 cup) caster (superfine) sugar
- 1 tbsp ground sumac
- 1 tbsp grated orange zest
- 3 eggs
- 280 g (10 oz/generous 1 cup) plain yoghurt
- 150 g (5½ oz/scant 1¼ cups) self-raising flour
- 160 g (5¾ oz/scant 1⅓ cups) semolina

For the syrup, pull the berries away from the flower heads and place in a saucepan. Pour over the measured boiling water and leave to infuse for 5 minutes before stirring in the sugar. Bring to the boil until the sugar has dissolved and the syrup is clear, then pour in the orange juice. Leave the sumac berries in the syrup as it cools down, before straining through a wide sieve (this will allow the flecks of sour sumac to pass through the sieve, but omit the berries).

Preheat the oven to 160°C (325°F/gas 3).

For the cake, place the butter, sugar, ground sumac and orange zest in a mixing bowl and beat until fluffy. Separate the eggs and slowly beat the yolks into the mixture (keep the whites to one side). Stir in the yoghurt and, once combined with the butter and sugar, gently fold in the flour and semolina.

In a separate bowl, whisk the egg whites until they form stiff peaks, then carefully fold into the cake batter (folding one spoonful through the batter first before adding the rest of the whites can help the egg white to integrate into the rest of the ingredients).

Spoon the batter into a greased and lined 20 cm (8 in) cake tin (pan) and bake for 30 minutes. Test with a skewer. If the top of the cake is turning brown but it hasn't cooked all the way through, place a heatproof plate on top of the cake tin and give it a further 10 minutes in the oven.

Remove from the oven and pierce all over the top of the cake with a skewer. Drizzle over the sumac syrup and leave to cool in the pan before removing and serving.

FLAVOUR PROFILE

LEAVES, BUDS AND FLOWERS
Perfumed · Slightly Bitter · Resinous

SEEDS Mild · Nutty
(the varieties with grey-and-white-striped seeds are most delicious)

SUNFLOWER HEART
Like perfumed artichoke

Sunflower

COMMONLY USED EDIBLE SPECIES

All species are edible.

WHERE THEY GROW

Most soils but prefers loose, well-drained soils. Plant in full sunlight where it will get at least 6–8 hours of direct sunlight each day.

WHEN TO GATHER

As soon as the seeds germinate you can harvest sunflowers as sprouting shoots. Gather the leaves and unopened flower buds in early summer, the immature flower heads in later summer, and ripe seeds and flower heads in early autumn (fall).

Along with germinating cress on a piece of damp cotton wool, sunflowers are one of the first seeds that children often have experience of growing – almost as a rite of passage, they push the large seeds into little pots of compost to watch seedlings emerge before taking their plants home. If they are lucky and don't forget about the little seedling in their bag, the seed can grow into a giant within a few months, towering over children and their parents with its large, flat flower head that turns its face to track the sun as it moves across the sky.

PARTS USED

① All parts of the plant are edible.

It's not only nursery children who plant sunflower seeds in the spring – for the last couple of hundred years, sunflowers have been sown in millions of acres of farmland across Eastern Europe. Huge fields of flowers in Ukraine, Romania and Russia produce most of the world's supply of oils for food and biofuel. So prolific are sunflowers across Eastern Europe that you might think that this is their place of origin, but they come from somewhere far more distant.

Sunflowers began their journey in the Americas. Wild sunflowers are a native prairie plant, far more delicate and ornamental than the sturdy giants we know today; growing through grasslands, they feature multiple flowers rather than the single bloom we are used to, but they are unmistakably sunflowers. As today, the seeds were eaten, pressed for oil and even ground into a seed flour to use in baking breads and sweetened cakes. In fact, across parts of North and South America, sunflowers were one of the first crops to be cultivated – the seeds taken from the wild and purposefully sown to grow for food, medicine, decoration and even dyes.

Not just a useful crop, they were also used for something far more esoteric – as a symbol of worship. Incan civilisations saw sunflowers as an earthly manifestation of their deity, the Sun God. Sunflower effigies were carved into temples and pressed into golden necklaces worn by priestesses. The Aztecs in Peru were no less devoted in their love of the sunflower, with similar golden adornments created in honour of the plant they named the 'shield flower'. The Mexican name for sunflower translates as 'big flower that looks at the sun'. Indeed, the sun-tracking phenomenon would've convinced even the most sceptical of souls that the flower on earth and the sun in the heavens were connected.

Sunflower's association with the worship of sun gods was so strong that some believe that the use of the plant by native people was suppressed by the Spanish when they invaded South America in an attempt to quash their culture and religions. Ironically, the invaders also fell under the sunflower's spell and took thousands of seeds back to Europe, where the plant was grown for a couple of hundred years purely for its sun-following beauty – its other uses were only discovered centuries after the flower spread across the continent.

Now you can spend hours driving though landscapes filled with sunflower crops, their heads turning to the west as the day progresses. The dominance of sunflowers in the landscape and as the source of an oil to fuel and feed the world came about more by chance than anything else. In a twist of fate, in the early days of growing the flower for food in Europe, the Orthodox Church devised a list of fats and oils that could not be eaten during Lent. Since sunflowers were still a rather niche crop and perhaps unknown to the author of the list, somehow they were omitted from it, thereby allowing people to cook food in the flower seed oil without breaking any laws of man or God. It may have been this sliding-doors moment that led the landscape of late-summer Eastern Europe to become what it is now: covered in flowers that symbolise devotion to a very different god to the one of the Orthodox Church, the oil-giving Sun God.

How to Process Sunflower Seeds

Place a handful of sunflower seeds in a bag, seal and lay it flat on a board, making sure that the seeds are in a single layer. Using a rolling pin, gently roll over the seeds to crack the shells (be warned this doesn't need brute force – too much pressure will squash the seeds). Once you've cracked the shells, shake the bag to start to separate the seeds from the shells.

Pour the contents of the bag into a bowl of water. The loose shells will rise to the surface of the water and can be scooped off and discarded. Gently rub the seeds in the water and the remainder of the shells should come away from the seeds. Scoop off and discard as before.

Drain and dry the seeds on a cloth or tea towel, before placing them on a baking sheet. Roast in an oven preheated to 180°C (350°F/gas 4) for 10–15 minutes, or until the seeds are golden. Store in an airtight jar for 3 months.

SERVES 4

Sunflower Heart Tarte Tatin

Sandwiched between the green base of the flower heads and the papery cups that hold the seed is a disc of soft, spongy flesh with a texture like aubergine (eggplant) that tastes more like a perfumed artichoke heart. To get access to your prized heart, remove any petals (set them aside for later) and pull off the seeds from the flower head (they should push out easily, but if they are resistant use a spoon to lever them out – keep the seeds to process later). Next, use a sharp knife to scrape the paper cases from the spongy base, discard them, and trim away the green parts of the flower head, including the leaves around the edge of the flower and where the stem joins underneath. You should be left with a round, white, slightly spongy base of the flower head. A small sunflower head will serve one person; a large head, two or three. Just like artichokes, sunflower hearts take time to prepare, and so deserve to be eaten with all the good things: and in this recipe, the good things they are paired with are butter, wine and pastry. You can make your own puff pastry, but after preparing the flowers you might be glad of some ready-to-roll.

- splash of olive oil
- 10 g (½ oz) butter
- 6 shallots, finely sliced
- pinch of salt
- 4 small or 2 large sunflower heads with petals
- 1 glass of white wine
- 2 tsp oregano leaves
- 2 tsp thyme leaves
- 1 x 320 g (11 oz) packet of puff pastry
- 25 g (1 oz) mature Cheddar cheese, finely grated

Heat the olive oil and butter in a sauté pan over a medium-low heat, add the shallots and salt, and sweat until they are turning golden, around 10 minutes. Remove from the heat and set aside.

Prepare your sunflower hearts as described above, reserving the petals for later. Slice the spongy bases into long strips and place in a bowl along with the wine and half of the oregano and thyme. Submerge the strips in the wine, ensuring they are covered or they will oxidise and go brown.

Return the pan of shallots to the hob, adding the sunflower strips, the wine and the remaining oregano and thyme leaves. Heat until the wine evaporates and the sunflower strips start to soften.

Line a round 32 cm (12 in) dish with baking parchment. Spoon the sunflower and onion mixture into the middle of the dish and leave to cool.

Meanwhile, preheat the oven to 180°C (350°F/gas 4).

When the filling is cool, roll out the puff pastry to the same size as the dish. Sprinkle the grated cheese over the cooled filling and carefully place the pastry disc on top, ensuring that all the ingredients are tucked inside. Press down the pastry and tuck in the edges around the outside of the filling. Prick a couple of holes in the centre to allow steam to escape.

Bake for 35–40 minutes, or until the pastry is golden.

Remove from the oven and let cool slightly before inverting the tart onto a serving platter. Peel back the baking parchment and scatter over the reserved sunflower petals.

Serve with a salad as a starter or main course.

Honey and Soy Roasted Sunflower Seeds

Sunflower seeds are a great, nutritious snack on their own, but with the addition of honey and soy they'll be reached for due to their moreishness, not just for their health benefits. Honey and soy-coated sunflower seeds are equally as delicious in a bowl with a beer, scattered over a herb salad or served on top of a bowl of soup.

MAKES 300 G (10½ OZ)

2 tbsp cold-pressed sunflower oil
300 g (10½ oz) sunflower seeds
2 tbsp honey
2 tbsp light soy sauce

Heat the sunflower oil in a frying pan over a low heat, add the seeds and toast for a couple of minutes, stirring the seeds frequently to make sure they don't burn. Remove from the heat, then stir in the honey and soy, making sure that the seeds are all covered in the sweet, salty mixture. Place the pan back on the heat and keep stirring until the liquid has all been absorbed and the seeds are glossy. Pour onto a non-stick baking sheet, or silicone mat to dry before spooning into airtight containers, where they can be stored for up to a couple of months.

Griddled Sunflower Heads

When sunflowers are in full bloom, their seeds are quietly growing under the plate of tiny yellow flowers. When they're first forming the seeds are soft like sweetcorn, and – just like corn – are delicious griddled on the barbecue.

To check if your sunflower is still at the tender stage, rub away a few of the little flowers and expose a few seeds – if they are small and creamy white, they are ideal for griddling.

SERVES 4

1 large or 4 small sunflower heads
2 tbsp olive oil
2 tbsp salted butter
1 garlic clove, crushed
a few sprigs of thyme

Heat a barbecue or griddle pan until hot. Rub away the small flowers from the top of the seeds on the sunflower head/s. Pull away the large petals (you can reserve these to use in salads).

In a bowl, mix together the olive oil, butter, garlic and the leaves from the thyme sprigs. Rub the olive oil and butter mixture onto the top of the flower head/s and place seed-side down onto the hot griddle or barbecue. Cook until the seeds are turning golden and soft.

If you have cooked a large flower head, slice it like pizza. Devour like corn on the cob.

SERVES 4

Sunflower Seed Tahini Dressing with Mixed Leaves, Grapes, Almonds and Parmesan

While true tahini is made with toasted sesame seeds, those who can't eat the tiny seeds but want to enjoy the indispensable paste may be glad to learn that sunflower seeds make a perfectly delicious alternative that can be used in hummus, halva and all other manner of recipes that require a dollop of the famous paste, including rich, creamy but sharp salad dressings (like this).

FOR THE SUNFLOWER TAHINI PASTE (MAKES A 250 G/9 OZ JAR)

150 g (5½ oz) hulled sunflower seeds
1 tbsp cold-pressed sunflower oil or olive oil
pinch of salt, or to taste

FOR THE DRESSING

50 g (1¾ oz) sunflower seed tahini (see above)
30 g (1 oz) plain yoghurt
1 garlic clove, crushed
2 tbsp light olive oil
juice of 1 lemon
1½ tsp maple syrup, or to taste
salt and black pepper

FOR THE SALAD

200g (7 oz) mustardy greens, such as wild rocket (arugula), watercress and red mustard, washed
100 g (3½ oz) sweet red grapes, halved
25 g (1 oz) toasted flaked (slivered) almonds
25 g (1 oz) toasted sunflower seeds
10 g (½ oz) Parmesan, shaved
sunflower petals, to garnish

For the sunflower tahini paste, preheat the oven to 180°C (350°F/gas 4).

Spread the seeds over a baking sheet. Place in the oven for 10–15 minutes until golden, shake the tray a couple of times whilst the seeds are cooking to ensure they toast evenly.

Place the toasted seeds in a blender and add 3 tablespoons of water. Blitz, slowly pouring in the oil until you get a smooth paste. Season with salt to taste and store in an airtight jar in the refrigerator.

To make the dressing, blend the sunflower seed tahini, yoghurt and garlic to a smooth purée, then stir in the olive oil, lemon juice and enough water to create a pourable sauce. Season with salt and pepper and enough maple syrup to sweeten to your taste.

Place the washed greens and half of the grapes, almonds and sunflower seeds into a large mixing bowl, pour over the dressing and toss through the salad, covering the leaves well. Spoon the dressed salad into a serving bowl and sprinkle with the remaining grapes, nuts and seeds, shaving over the fresh Parmesan. Serve immediately as a side salad or alone as a light lunch.

FLAVOUR PROFILE Earthy · Bitter · Antiseptic · Sweet · Floral

Saffron

COMMONLY USED EDIBLE SPECIES

Crocus sativus (saffron crocus).

WHERE THEY GROW

Plant your corms (bulbs) in well-drained, fertile soil in full sun or light shade. Saffron does not grow well in acidic soils; if your soil is acidic, grow the corms in pots.

WHEN TO GATHER

Late autumn (fall).

Saffron is, as everyone knows, the world's most expensive spice – gram for gram, it is even more valuable than gold. You've probably seen and tasted the incredible effects a few strands of the dried stamens have on food – lacing it with an earthy, almost antiseptic flavour and turning whatever you eat to a golden yellow colour. Quite how so much colour and flavour comes from the thread-like stamens beggars belief, and yet somehow someone saw the potential in those tiny threads. That someone lived at least 50,000 years ago, when cave paintings located in what is now Iraq were created using wild saffron stamens as a pigment – most likely it was just ground up and its yellow colouring infused into water or fats.

PARTS USED

① Stamen
② Petals (used in teas)

CAUTION

It is very important not to confuse saffron with *Colchicum autumnale* (also known as autumn crocus, meadow saffron or naked ladies). This is a fatally toxic plant in flower at the same time as saffron crocus. *Colchicum* are similar to saffron, but have larger flowers and strappy clusters of leaves that grow in the spring but die back by the autumn (fall). Only ever harvest saffron from corms you have planted. Do not plant saffron corms near a patch of *Colchicum* to avoid any confusion and never harvest saffron from the wild in case you have the wrong plant.

The fashion for using saffron wasn't a fleeting affair; 45,000 years later the plant itself was featured in positively modern wall paintings in Crete and Santorini – both frescos showed people gathering their saffron harvests. By the time of the Greco-Roman world, wild saffron was cultivated, and bred into the saffron we know today – *Crocus sativus* was created. At that point, it wasn't just used as a paint or a flavouring, but was also used by physicians as a medicine, Cleopatra bathed in it (infused into her famous donkey-milk baths) and traders sold it.

Those traders were initially the Phoenicians, a collective of sea-faring people who straddled the Mediterranean coastline, establishing the first ports and sea-trading posts that would become the iconic routes for spices to travel along. Amongst them was saffron, which was spread by trading for items as varied as cloth and metal, including sought-after tin – a vital ingredient in making bronze. Tin was in plentiful supply on the Cornish coast of Britain and at some point there was a fortuitous swap between the Phoenicians and the Cornish tin traders, exchanging their precious metal for the spice more valuable than gold. Over the years, the demand for saffron in Britain and Northern Europe grew, until in the Middle Ages they too became home to saffron harvests. Farmland turned purple in the autumn (fall) as agricultural workers who might've been more used to gathering barley and rye bent over gathering the millions of saffron strands by hand. But farming fashions change and, perhaps fortunately for the European harvesters' backs, saffron became cheaper to import from other countries. Now there are only a few saffron farms so far north – the majority of the world's harvest is grown in Iran, where every year over 230 metric tons of the tiny stamens are harvested and dried – literally billons of threads, all hand-plucked from the flowers as they open each November, dried and cured before they are packed into millions of tiny 1 g pots and sent across the world to colour and flavour food. The saffron that isn't exported is put to very good use as a flavouring and colouring for rice dishes, stews, soups and, of course, sweeter treats, including *bastani sonnati* (saffron ice cream) and delicious tahini brittles.

If you want to have an annual saffron harvest in your own home but don't live in a warm climate, take heart from the old farms of chilly northern Europe, because saffron is a hardy little flower. A dozen or so corms will not only give you a gram of your own-grown saffron, but will provide a splash of much-needed colour when other plants are going into hibernation. Once you've gathered and dried your saffron, to make the best of the tiny filaments, cast your memory back to how the cave painters of Iraq turned the threads into paint: by pounding and infusing them in water. If you have the inclination to add another step in your saffron-extraction process, wrap your strands in a foil parcel and gently heat them in a pan for a few seconds before pounding and infusing them. This will ensure you extract every last vestige of colour and hint of flavour from the spice. And, of course, if you have any left you could always find yourself a cave to paint.

How to Process Saffron

Saffron flowers bloom for a few weeks in autumn, providing a late burst of regal colour in a fading garden. After a couple of years, an initial planting of a couple of dozen corms will yield enough saffron stamens to satisfy a personal annual supply of the spice. Each year the plants produce new corms and within a few years you will become a saffron smallholder, with enough spices to trade with a few friends and jealous neighbours.

You have two ways to harvest: if you are a proud gardener and want to hold onto your floral display, you can pluck just the stamens from the plants, leaving the flowers to be admired. If you'd prefer to avoid the bending to pluck the tiny stamens and you're happy to lose your flowers, pluck the whole flower and head to the kitchen to remove the stamens. However you harvest, remember to gather your stamens the day the flowers have just opened, ideally in the morning before direct sunlight has drained the best flavour from them.

Not only are they at their peak in the first morning of opening, the stamens are also easier to extract whole at this stage, meaning you will gain more flavour and quantity. Use a pair of tweezers to gently pull the three stamens from each flower. If you're doing this outside, place the threads into a small jar to stop them blowing away in a gust of wind. Once inside, lay the saffron on a piece of paper towel or fine cloth such as a piece of stretched silk, then cover with another layer of cloth or paper to stop the strands from flying away while they are dehydrating. Dry the saffron on the lowest setting of a dehydrator or by a warm radiator. When the strands are brittle, place them in an airtight jar and ideally store for 30 days before using to allow the flavours to develop.

SERVES 6

Cauliflower and Saffron Pie

B'stillas are sweet savoury pies made for special occasions, traditionally flavoured with saffron and filled with squab pigeons, dried fruit and rice. If your celebrations don't involve eating squabs, cauliflower is just as at home encased in fruit, spices and filo pastry.

- drizzle of olive oil
- 1 large sweet onion, finely sliced
- ¼ tsp ground cinnamon
- 100 g (3½ oz/genrous ¾ cup) raisins
- 100 g (3½ oz/⅔ cup) pine nuts
- 100 g (3½ oz/generous 1 cup) flaked (slivered) almonds
- 2 tsp honey
- 0.2 g (½ packet) saffron, toasted (see page 235) and all but a few strands soaked in 250 ml (8½ fl oz/1 cup) hot water
- 250 g (9 oz) cauliflower florets, coarsely blitzed into small pieces (slightly bigger than you'd make cauliflower rice)
- 6 sheets of filo pastry
- melted butter (or oil), for brushing
- 1 tsp nigella seeds
- 2 tsp icing (confectioners') sugar
- salt, to taste

Heat a drizzle of olive oil in a saucepan over a medium heat, add the onion and sweat until golden, seasoning with a pinch of salt and the cinnamon. Add the raisins, pine nuts and almonds, and stir through the honey, then set aside.

Pour the saffron-infused water into a saucepan with a lid and bring to a simmer, then add the cauliflower, coating all the pieces in the saffron water. Put a lid on the pan for 1 minute, then remove from the heat and cool the contents by placing the bottom of the pan in a large bowl of cold water (this stops the cauliflower from overcooking and losing its flavour). Leave the cauliflower to soak in the saffron liquid.

Preheat the oven to 160°C (325°F/gas 3).

Line a 20 cm (8 in) cake tin (pan) with the filo pastry sheets, brushing each sheet with melted butter and placing each sheet off centre in the tin so that half of each sheet is on the bottom of the tin and the rest hangs over the edge of the tin like petals around a flower head.

Strain the cauliflower in a sieve (strainer). (Reserve the saffron liquid – this could be added to a potato soup, for instance.) Mix the cauliflower with the onion, fruit and nut mix, and spoon the mixture into the filo-lined tin. Pull the overhanging pastry together into a bundle, brush with a little of the saffron water and remaining butter, then sprinkle with nigella seeds and salt.

Bake in the oven for 40–45 minutes until golden.

Pound the remaining saffron strands with the icing sugar, until the icing turns bright yellow.

Remove from the oven and dust the pie with the saffron icing sugar before serving hot or at room temperature.

Moorish Saffron Meat Skewers

The histories of saffron and Moorish food go hand in hand. In Spain, these *pinchos morunos* have Moorish origins (the name translates to 'Moorish skewers'). The meat – usually pork or chicken, is marinated in numerous spices, including saffron, to make the very best of kebabs.

SERVES 4

500 g (1 lb 2 oz) cubed pork or chicken
2 garlic cloves, crushed
1 tsp smoked paprika
1 tsp dried oregano
½ tsp ground coriander
½ tsp ground cumin
½ tsp ground fennel
½ tsp salt
¼ tsp saffron, infused in 2 tbsp boiled water for 20 minutes
1 bay leaf, crumbled (or pinch of dried bay leaf powder)
2 tbsp red wine vinegar
2 tsp olive oil

Place all the ingredients in a bowl and rub the mixture thoroughly into the meat, making sure that all pieces are well coated. Cover, place in the refrigerator and leave to marinate overnight.

The next day, push the marinated meat onto skewers and cook on a hot griddle or barbecue, turning until cooked through. Serve with a couscous salad or stuffed into breads.

Sohan-e Qom Persian Brittle

Originating in the Iranian holy city of Qom, saffron brittle is a sweet, crisp candy made with tahini and sugar.

MAKES 20 PIECES

200 g (7 oz/scant 1 cup) granulated sugar
150 g (5½ oz/scant ⅔ cup) tahini paste
½ tsp saffron, soaked in 2 tbsp hot water for 20 minutes
handful of chopped pistachios

Line a lipped baking sheet with oiled greaseproof paper or a silicone liner.

Place a heavy-based pan over a very low heat, add the sugar and slowly heat until it melts and starts to bubble and caramelise, reaching 130°C (300°F) or cracking stage. Once the sugar has started to brown, mix the tahini with the saffron-infused water and stir into the melted sugar.

Pour the mixture into the prepared baking sheet and scatter with the pistachios, pressing them into the mixture. Refrigerate until set before snapping and storing in an airtight container for up to a couple of weeks (if you can resist eating it all before then!).

MAKES 10

Saffron Buns

Cornwall is a place built on trade with the sea; its rich seam of tin was one of the most important elements in turning copper into bronze and the first seafaring Phoenicians sailed from the saffron-scented Middle East to the rugged Cornish shores to buy the precious metal. Some historians think this is when saffron first arrived in Cornwall – whether they are right or not, saffron is as saturated in its food as its people are in the salty sea. And saffron buns are a sweet reminder of the rich trading history of the land of the Cornish.

- 0.5 g (1 packet) saffron strands
- 100 g (3½ oz/scant ½ cup) golden caster (superfine) sugar
- 400 ml (14 fl oz/generous 1½ cups) whole milk
- 50 g (1¾ oz) unsalted butter, softened
- 550 g (1 lb 4 oz/scant 4½ cups) strong white bread flour, sifted
- 1 x 7 g (¼ oz) sachet of fast-action dried yeast
- 1 tsp sea salt
- 100 g (3½ oz/generous ¾ cup) raisins
- 1 egg, beaten (mixed with a little milk), for brushing

The flavours of saffron are released through toasting, pounding and soaking. Place the saffron in the centre of a small square of kitchen foil, fold the foil into a parcel around the saffron, forming a tight seal, then place the parcel in a hot dry pan for 30 seconds. This will toast the saffron without burning it.

Pour the toasted saffron into a pestle and mortar and add a couple of pinches of the sugar to act as an abrasive. Pound the sugar and saffron to a powder.

Heat the milk in a saucepan until just before it boils. Remove from the heat and pour most of the saffron sugar into the hot milk (retain a small amount to add to a syrup glaze later). Add the butter and stir until the butter is dissolved, then set aside for 20 minutes.

Combine the flour, half of the sugar, the yeast and salt in a large bowl. Pour the infused milk onto the dry ingredients and use a knife to blend the ingredients together, then knead for at least 5 minutes. Leave the dough to rest for a few minutes before adding the raisins, then knead again until the dough is smooth and springy. Cover the bowl with a damp, clean dish towel and place somewhere warm until the dough has doubled in size (about 30 minutes–1 hour).

When the dough has risen, knead it again for a minute, before dividing the dough into 10 equal pieces. Form each piece into a little ball. Place the balls on a lined baking tray, leaving a little space between them to allow for expansion. Cover again and leave to rise for 20 minutes.

Preheat the oven to 200°C (400°F/gas 6).

Once risen, brush the buns with the egg and milk mixture and bake for 20 minutes, or until golden.

Meanwhile, dissolve the remaining sugar in a pan with 3 tablespoons of water and add the leftover saffron/sugar mix. Simmer until the sugar dissolves and leave over a low heat to reduce slightly.

When the buns are cooked, drizzle them with the golden syrup and leave to cool before serving. Serve with butter or clotted cream.

FLAVOUR PROFILE

TUBERS Nutty · Sweet · Root vegetable flavour, similar to Jerusalem artichoke

LEAF SHOOTS Mild · Similar to water chestnut

FLOWERS Pepper · Carrot · Cabbage · Garlic · Onion · Radish

Day Lily

COMMONLY USED EDIBLE SPECIES

Hemerocallis fulva (orange or tiger day lily), *Hemerocallis citrina* (citron day lily), *Hemerocallis middendorffii* (amur day lily), *Hemerocallis dumortieri* (dumorties day lily), *Hemerocallis lilioasphodelus* (yellow day lily), *Hemerocallis minor* (dwarf day lily).

WHERE THEY GROW

Day lilies grow in most conditions, tolerating all soil conditions and climates. They need to be in full sun to produce many flowers.

WHEN TO GATHER

Tubers – winter–spring

Shoots – spring

Flowers – summer

Take a trip to an Southeast Asian supermarket and you'll probably come across a packet of yellow day lily flower buds, plucked before they open and dried before being shipped across the world to be used in Southeast Asian recipes in lands far from its origin.

PARTS USED

① Tubers
② Young shoots
③ Flower buds, flowers

Day lily's name and the shape of the flower when it is in bloom might lead you to think that you're looking at a plant from the lily family, but you'd have been led up the wrong garden path if you do. Although the flowers of day lilies look like lilies, they're actually part of a different family of plants, the *Asphodelaceae*, which is also home to red hot pokers, aloes and succulents. True lilies grow from bulbs, but if you dig up a day lily plant you'll see it grows from a cluster of tubers which look almost like a bunch of deflated balloons – rhizomes. And it is important to get to know how to identify day lily because many true lilies are toxic, while day lily is a delicious, long-eaten plant – hence the packets of dried flowers in the supermarket.

Just as you might find packets of dried day lily flowers in your local Southeast Asian food store, you'll probably have a plant growing somewhere near you, since day lily is common the world over. Native to East Asia, it spread across the world along the Silk Road before finding its way into gardens across Europe, and eventually onto ships bound for America in the 19th century. If you have day lily plants in your garden, you might be wondering quite why this plant was given precious space on long sea voyages, since its flowers open, bloom and wilt within a single day. But day lily is an incredibly hardy plant and even the least green-fingered gardener would've been able to make it thrive in their flower bed. And thrive they did, soon taking root in their new home, they spread across the eastern parts of America becoming part of the notorious list of invasive species.

Where day lilies are invasive in America you'll often find advice to dig up the rhizomes. It can be back-breaking work digging up huge clumps of day lilies, but take inspiration from the plant's homelands and turn your uprooting into a harvest, especially if you dig up the plants in winter or early spring when the new shoots appear. New growth day lily stems are a lovely early spring green – mild and crunchy, they are delicious braised like leeks in butter and wine sauces as they absorb the flavour of everything. And it's not just the shoots that make good eating – the tubers are sweet and utterly delicious, their flavour reminiscent of Jerusalem artichoke. In fact, many fans of day lily tubers claim that they are the best root vegetable around (they're definitely the best invasive root vegetable you'll dig up).

Don't go digging all your plants up though, because later in the summer you will discover why Southeast Asian supermarkets sell packets of the dried flowers – and once you do you'll probably want more of the plant in your garden. Day lily flower buds are packed full of flavours, with hints of carrot, radish, cabbage, garlic and chilli. They're a treat eaten fresh in the summer or dried for use through the winter. The unapologetically savoury flowers are a key ingredient in East Asian cookery where for thousands of years they have been grown, harvested and eaten as food and medicine. Rich in vitamins A and B, and minerals including phosphorus, calcium and iron, day lily flowers are farmed and widely used in China, Japan, Korea, Taiwan, Siberia and Myanmar, both to add flavour and to thicken dishes. Day lily buds are most famously used in hot and sour soups, or in fermented vegetable dishes. If you have an abundance of flower buds, harvest some before they bloom, to dry, ferment, or dip in batter and tempura. You can also harvest the flowers when they have had their day of blooming. Add them to stir-fries, or dry and use just like the packets of day lilies– just with far fewer food miles.

CAUTIONARY NOTE

However you eat day lily, it is worth taking note of a couple of things: firstly, the translation of its Chinese name means 'the shrub that makes you forget'; eaten raw in a large quantity day lily is reputed to be a sedative and slightly hallucinogenic – this is especially the case with the leaves, so if you eat them make sure you cook them first. Secondly, while day lily is a widely eaten food, a few people have a reaction to them, so – like any new food – introduce them slowly to your diet and make sure you are harvesting from one of the recommended edible species rather than from a cultivar.

SERVES 4

Day Lily Tuber Gratin

Like Jerusalem artichokes, day lily tubers contain a gut-health-supporting prebiotic starch called inulin; and like Jerusalem artichoke, day lily tubers cook into delicious gratins. A word to the wise when serving this gratin – inulin is incredibly good for you, but when you first introduce it to your diet, it has a reputation for making the next day rather windy. If you're concerned about the following day, reduce the amount of day lily tubers, adding more potato.

250 g (9 oz) day lily tubers
1 kg (2 lb 4 oz) potatoes
juice of ½ lemon
20 g (¾ oz) butter
2 leeks, finely sliced into discs
1 garlic clove, crushed
½ tsp ground fennel
1 tsp fresh thyme
20 g (¾ oz) Parmesan cheese, grated
200 ml (7 fl oz/scant 1 cup) double (heavy) cream
100 ml (3½ fl oz/scant ½ cup) chicken or vegetable stock
100 g (3½ oz) Cheddar cheese, grated
salt and black pepper, to taste

Preheat the oven to 220°C (425°F/gas 7).

Thoroughly wash and scrub the day lily tubers and potatoes. Use the edge of a spoon or a vegetable peeler to scrape away the thin tuber skins, thinly slice the potatoes and cut the day lily tubers in half and place them in a bowl of water with the lemon juice squeezed in (this prevents them from turning brown).

Heat the butter in a saucepan, then add the leeks and sauté until softened. Add the garlic, ground fennel and half of the fresh thyme, and cook for a further 5 minutes over a low heat until the leeks just start turning golden.

Transfer the leek mixture to an ovenproof casserole dish, spreading it evenly across the base. Drain the day lily tubers and potatoes and dry them on a dish towel, layering the tubers and potatoes on top of the leeks. Sprinkle over the remaining thyme along with the Parmesan and season with salt and pepper.

In a separate bowl, mix together the cream and stock, then pour over the gratin, pressing down any pieces of tuber or potato that might be sticking up above the liquid. Sprinkle over the grated Cheddar and bake in the oven for 30 minutes, or until the day lily and potato have softened.

Delicious served with sausages and leafy greens.

SERVES 4

Day Lily Soup with Chicken

Day lily flowers are a key ingredient in traditional Chinese hot and sour soup – the fiery, sinus-clearing medicinal dish laden with vinegar and white pepper. Adding the creamy tubers and mild new stems turns what is a bowl of sour heat into something more cosy but equally nourishing. (If you want to turn up the dial on the heat and sourness, add more pepper and vinegar.)

- 15 g (½ oz) dried shiitake mushrooms
- 10 g (scant ½ oz) dried day lily flowers
- 15 g (½ oz) dried wood ear mushrooms (known as black fungus in Chinese supermarkets)
- 1 litre (34 fl oz/4¼ cups) good-quality chicken or vegetable stock
- 2 tsp finely grated fresh root ginger
- 2 large spring onions (scallions), thinly sliced
- 100g (3½ oz) firm tofu, diced into small cubes
- shredded cooked chicken pieces (use more tofu if not adding chicken)
- 20 g (¾ oz) bamboo shoots, cut into julienne (tinned is fine)
- 20 g (¾ oz) day lily tubers, peeled and sliced into thin batons
- 4 tbsp light soy sauce
- 20 g (¾ oz/2½ tbsp) cornflour (cornstarch)
- handful of day lily shoots (or the base of the plant if gathered in summer), sliced into thin discs
- 4 tbsp Chinese black vinegar or rice wine vinegar
- 1 tsp white pepper (or ground black pepper)
- 2 eggs, beaten
- 1 tsp sesame oil

Place the dried shiitake and day lily flowers into a bowl and cover with water (at least 600ml/20 fl oz/2½ cups). Place the wood ear mushrooms in a separate bowl and cover with water. Leave the mushrooms and flowers for a couple of hours to rehydrate before removing them from their liquid (reserve the liquid from the shiitake and day lily mix). Finely slice the mushrooms and cut off the woody end of the flowers.

Pour the chicken or vegetable stock and 500 ml (17 fl oz/generous 2 cups) of the reserved soaking liquid into a saucepan, add the ginger and spring onions, bring to a simmer and cook for 10 minutes. Add the mushrooms, day lily flowers, tofu, chicken, bamboo shoots, day lily tubers and soy sauce, and simmer for a further 2 minutes.

Spoon a few tablespoons of the stock into a bowl with the cornflour and mix to a smooth paste; pour this into the soup, stirring until the soup becomes glossy and very slightly thickened. Add the finely sliced day lily shoots, vinegar and white pepper, then taste and add more vinegar for sourness and pepper for heat, as preferred. Turn the heat down to the lowest setting to keep the soup warm.

Just before serving, swirl the beaten egg through the soup. When the egg is cooked, ladle the soup into bowls and serve with a drizzle of the sesame oil.

How to Dry Day Lily Flowers

Chinese food stores sell bags of dried day lily buds – they are prized for their earthy, peppery flavour. Day lily flowers bloom over a few weeks, each flowering stem has a number of buds that follow in succession one after the other, blooming for a day before they wilt and dry on the plant. Traditionally, day lily buds are collected before they open for their day of display, but if you want to have your cake and eat it, you can let the flower open, admire its orange blossom throughout the day, and cut off the flower in the evening. Freshly harvested and dried open flowers taste every bit as delicious as store-bought, old buds.

You can process the flowers in two ways: either drying them in a dehydrator straight away, or by soaking them for 48 hours in a salt brine solution before draining, drying and dehydrating. The second method results in a more complex flavour.

Either way, when you dehydrate the flowers, they act in a very similar way to roses and rehydrate with moisture quickly. Make sure your flowers are dried to a crumbling consistency and that you jar them immediately after dehydrating. Dried day lily buds will keep for at least a year.

Day Lily Flower and Sesame Salad

Day lily flowers are used in salads, stir-fries and pickles in Southeast Asian cookery. This salad is equally moreish served cold or stir-fried with slivers of pork or tofu.

SERVES 4

FOR THE DRESSING

1 tbsp rice wine vinegar
2 tsp sesame oil
½ red chilli
1½ tsp sugar
½ tsp salt
pinch of white pepper

FOR THE SALAD

50 g (1¾ oz) fresh or soaked day lily buds
1 carrot
½ cucumber
½ mooli radish (or turnip)
½ red pepper
2 tsp toasted sesame seeds

If using dehydrated day lily buds, soak them in water for 1 hour, or until softened.

Place the dressing ingredients in a jar and shake until combined. Keep tasting until it has taken on enough heat from the chilli. Once the dressing is at your preferred level of heat, remove the chilli.

Finely julienne the carrot, cucumber, mooli and pepper into thin sticks the length of the day lily buds. Cut off the woody ends of the day lily buds and slice the flowers into 4 lengthways. Place all of the vegetables in a bowl and pour over the dressing, stirring to cover all of the ingredients. Scatter with toasted sesame seeds before serving.

Day lily salad is delicious served with soy-glazed pork chops or stirred through noodles. You can also turn any remaining salad into a stir-fry by flash-frying leftovers in a wok.

Day Lily and Chinese Leaf Kimchi

Day lily flower buds have an uncanny taste of kimchi about them, with hints of hot garlic, cabbage and carrot, so it's not a big jump to turn them into the thing they taste of – a sour, tangy, microbe-rich Korean kimchi, suitable for the healthiest of salads or to be dolloped onto the fattiest of beef burgers.

MAKES 1 LITRE
(34 FL OZ/4¼ CUPS) JAR

750 g (1 lb 10 oz) Chinese leaf (napa cabbage), shredded
100 g (3½ oz) day lily flower buds, cut into discs
30 g (1 oz/¼ cup) salt
3 garlic cloves
1½ tsp coarsely grated fresh root ginger
2 tbsp Korean chilli flakes
1 tbsp fish sauce
1 tsp sugar
1 bunch of spring onions (scallions), finely sliced

Place the cabbage and day lily buds in a bowl and rub thoroughly with the salt. Cover with cold water and leave for at least 30 minutes until the cabbage starts to soften, although this may take up to a couple of hours. Rinse the cabbage and day lily buds under cold running water, then drain thoroughly and dry in a dish towel. Place in a bowl.

In a pestle and mortar, blend the garlic, ginger, chilli flakes, sugar and fish sauce into a paste and massage it into the cabbage, buds and spring onion, ensuring they are well covered. Then spoon them into a clean jar, pressing every layer down firmly to press out as much air as possible. Submerge them under their own liquid with a fermenting stone or a bag full of water.

Leave in a cool place away from sunlight for 5 days, checking on the kimchi regularly, making sure that the vegetables are submerged and tasting it for flavour. When the kimchi is sour and tangy, place it in the refrigerator to slow down the fermentation, where it will keep for up to a month.

ACKNOWLEDGEMENTS

To my lovely husband and children, dogs and cat. Thank you for being the heart of my home. I might adore the plants in the garden, but I love you all more (even if three of you do spend your lives trying to dig up everything I have ever grown.)

A few years ago, when I wrote my first book, I was paired with the most patient of editors – Chelsea Edwards. She edited my book through the first Covid lockdown – as I juggled home schooling, and writing deadlines, hers was one of the few faces I'd see other than my family's. When the book was finished I missed Chelsea's virtual presence, grammar correcting and text chasing probably more than most writers miss being 'hounded' by their editors. Thank you Chelsea for asking me to work with you again, I've loved it. This time around, I've been blessed by another very patient editor, Emily Preece-Morrison. Thank you Emily for your eye for detail and for making *Buds & Blossoms* a far better book than it would've been without you.

I discovered writing this that an illustrated book comes with a whole other team of people – photographer, food stylist, props coordinators and cooks, and for the most glorious few days all these wonderful people came together in little studios to turn my recipes into food. We sat and ate the dishes you see in the pages – lunches on shoot days were piles of floral meringues, stem-filled soups, sunflower tarts and rose petal pastas. Not only did the food go together, so did the team and between them they created (and ate) the beautiful photos in the book. Thank you Esther, Claire, Kim, Marie and Rachel. I loved every moment of the shoots with you all – my memories of working with you on this book are filed under 'soul food'.

Many of the plants photographed in this book were grown by neighbours and friends: the water lily came from my friends Sue and Ian Mabberly's pond, lilac from my neighbour Tracie's pot-grown shrub, sumac from a garden lining the local village street, cherry blossom from a nearby smallholding, and the sunflowers, picked from a garden full of the giant sun-following flowers, which were planted by the children who live there and adored by anyone who passes by. Thank you for allowing me to eat your gardens – they were delicious.

Thank you to the gardeners who came before – to my grandparents for growing roses that filled my memories with scent. To Cath and Vic, who fed me edible fuchsias and opened my eyes to what food can be, thank you for taking time out of your day to feed a little girl's curiosity for the world. To people I didn't know but whose decision to plant what they did has made the world that bit more beautiful, including the 1940s street planners of Letchworth who lined Lammas Way with ornamental cherries – you provided the most magical of walks to primary school a child could have.

Finally, thanks to you for buying or borrowing this book – I hope it inspires you to look at the plants around you in a new, delicious way – and perhaps add some new plants to your garden, you never know, in 100 years' time someone might pluck a flower from them and wonder whether its delicious scent could be edible.

ABOUT THE AUTHOR

When she was a child, Liz was given an edible Fuchsia berry to eat by a knowledgeable older friend – one bite into the peppery, plump fruit (which tasted of kiwi, fig and plum) was enough to make her start to wonder whether the plants that grew around her were more than just flowers or weeds.

It turned out that lots were, and Liz now spends her days teaching people about the food that surrounds us – some of these are wild plants, and others are the blousy ornamentals that fill our garden beds.

Over the years, Liz has sold her floral foods to food halls including Fortnum and Mason and taught thousands of people during foraging walks and demonstrations. Liz has appeared on a number of television programs including her regular wild food slot on Channel 5's Escape To the Farm with Kate Humble, where basketfuls of flowers were regularly eaten and enjoyed. *Buds & Blossoms* is Liz's second cookbook.

Index

A

B

C

D

E

F

R

S

T

V

W

Y

Z

More Plants to Grow and Eat

If the 20 plants featured in *Buds & Blossoms* have got you wondering what other beautiful, edible plants you could grow, and how you could use them, here are a few more that you could make space for in your garden.

BOTANICAL NAME	COMMON NAME (UK)	PARTS USED	FLAVOUR PROFILE	HOW TO USE
Acorus calamus	Sweet Flag	Roots · Stems	ROOTS Gingery LEAVES Lemony STALKS Vanilla	Use in small amounts as spice to flavour foods
Albizia julibrissin	Mimosa tree	Young leaves · Flowers	Sour · Astringent	Leaves as a vegetable, flowers in drinks, preserves and garnishes
Agastache	Anise hyssop	Leaves · Flowers	Lemon · Anise	As a herbal flavouring in drinks and cooking
Alcea rosea	Holly hock	Roots · Leaves · Flowers · Seeds	Mild · Mucilaginous	Leaves used as a vegetable, the roots as a thickener, flowers in drinks and salads – stuff large flowers as you would courgettes (zucchini)
Althaea Officinalis	Marsh mallow	Roots · Leaves · Flowers · Seeds	Mild · Mucilaginous	Leaves used as a vegetable, the roots as a thickener, flowers in drinks and salads
Amaranthus caudatus	Love lies bleeding	Leaves · Seeds	Spinachy leaves · Nutty seeds	Use as a vegetable, the leaves as a grain in soups, stews and baking
Begonia Tuberhybrida	Tuberous begonia	Flowers · Stems	Sour · Fruity	In desserts, salads and as a garnish for tagines/ spiced dishes
Campanula	Bellflowers	Flowers	Mild · Fresh	Added to salads or as a garnish for sweet and savoury dishes
Canna	Canna lily	Leaves · Tubers	Mild leaves · Water chestnut-like tubers	Eat the leaves as a vegetable or wrap (like Hosta) the tubers like Day Lily tubers
Calycanthus	Carolina allspice	Bark	Cinnamon spiced flavour when dried	Use as a substitute for cinnamon
Centaurea cyanus	Cornflower	Flowers · Leaves · Young shoots	Mild · Faintly earthy	The flowers and leaves are used in herbal teas; flowers as garnish and salad ingredient, the leaves as a vegetable
Cercis	Red bud tree	Flowers · Seed pods · Young leaves	Sour · Fruity	Flower buds make great pickles, the flowers, leaves and seed pods can be eaten raw or cooked
Chaenomeles japonica	Japanese quince	Flowers · Fruits	FLOWERS Fruity · Sour FRUIT Perfumed (like quince) · Sour	Use the flowers in place of Camellia flowers in winter salads, in syrups or as a garnish. The fruits make wonderful jams and liqueurs

BOTANICAL NAME	COMMON NAME (UK)	PARTS USED	FLAVOUR PROFILE	HOW TO USE
Chrysanthemum	Chrysanthemum	Leaves · Flowers	Herbal · Aromatic · Slightly bitter	Sweat young shoots in oil; add to soups Flowers in salads (similar flavour to Marigold and Sunflower)
Dahlia	Dahlia	Flowers · Tubers	FLOWERS Mild to spicy TUBERS Water chestnut like texture, ranging from fruity to spicy flavours	Use Dahlia flowers in salads and baking, the roots can be used like Day Lily roots
Dianthus Caryophyllus	Carnation	Flowers	Sweet clove · Nutmeg	Use in syrups, liqueurs and baking – lovely with cream puddings
Eschscholzia	California poppy	Flowers · Leaves	Bitter	Most frequently used to make soothing teas, flowers in salads and garnishes, or to make bitters. Leaves cooked
Forsythia	Forsythia	Flowers	Bitter · Perfumed	Syrups, cocktails, teas, salad
Fuschia	Fuschia	Fruits · Flowers	FRUIT Figgy · Plummy · Mildly peppery FLOWERS Mild	Raw or cooked as fruits, preserved as jams and chutneys. The flowers are beautiful garnishes
Freesia	Freesia	Flowers	Sweet · Perfumed	Infused into syrups like jasmine and used to flavour desserts and drinks
Gardenia jasminoides	Cape jasmine	Flowers · Leaves · Fruit	FLOWERS Lemony · Peachy · Bitter FRUITS Slightly LEAVES Fruit bitter	Leaves to make tea (like Camellia) Flowers infused into syrups and liqueurs – can be used like Camellia Fruit is rich in carotenoids and will turn food yellow
Gladiolus	Gladioli	Flowers	Mild · Similar to lettuce	Use in salads, stuffed as a canapé
Hesperis matronalis	Dame's rocket / Sweet rocket	Leaves · Flowers · Buds · Flowers · Seeds	Sweet · Floral · Cabbage · Slightly spicy · Mild leaves (part of the cabbage family)	Leaves: wilted like spinach. Flowers buds fried in butter Flowers in salads
Hibiscus sabdariffa	Hibiscus	Flowers · Fruits · Calyx leaves	Sour · Fruity · Tangy · Rhubarb like	All parts in salads, stews, drinks and syrups. The calyx used to colour food and make syrups
Hylotelephium spectabile	Sedum	Leaves · Young flower heads (best in bud)	Refreshing · Crunchy · Sour · Slightly bitter · A good carrier of other flavours	Raw, stir-fried, pickled or cooked in butter and wine and sauces
Impatiens walleriana	Busy Lizzie	Flowers	Sweet	Salads, desserts, garnishes for drinks and cakes
Lobularia	Alyssum	Flowers · Leaves	Honeyed · Mustard (part of the cabbage family)	Salads, finely chopped into salsas or garnishes for desserts
Lonicera japonica	Japanese honeysuckle	Flowers	Perfumed · Sweet · Floral	Infused into drinks, syrups and vinegars. Add honeysuckle to savoury dishes with soy, ginger and garlic

BOTANICAL NAME	COMMON NAME (UK)	PARTS USED	FLAVOUR PROFILE	HOW TO USE
Lunaria annua	Honesty	Flowers · Tubers · Seed pods · Seeds	FLOWERS Sweet · Slightly peppery SEEDS Similar to wasabi TUBERS Turnipy	Flowers in salads, stir-fry the tubers, use the seeds in salads for a peppery bite, seeds infused into vinegar, scattered into salads, or dried and ground as a spice
Mahonia aquifolium	Oregon Grape	Berries · Flowers	Very sour berries · Sherbet · Lemon flowers	Use in drinks, syrups, jellies and jams. Add the flowers to desserts like lemon tarts
Muscari	Grape hyacinth	Flowers	Bitter · Perfumed	In bitters, garnishes
Malva	Mallow	Roots · Leaves · Flowers · Stems	Slimy · Mild · Creamy	Grind the roots to use as a thickener, leaves in salads and cooked as a vegetable. Flowers in salads and sweet dishes
Nigella sativa & Damascena	Black cumin and Love in a mist	Seeds · Flowers in moderation	Smoky spiced *sativa* seeds are sold as spice nigella. Damascena (love in a mist) has milder seeds	As a spice
Orchidaceae Dendrobium	Orchid	Flowers · Leaves · Shoots · Pseudo roots	FLOWERS Mild · Lettuce ROOTS Sweet	Flowers in salads and as a garnish for drinks and desserts. The roots of certain orchids can be ground up as a seasoning known as salep
Osmanthus fragrans	Sweet osmanthus	Flowers · Leaves	FLOWERS Fruity · Sweet · Slightly bitter LEAVES Mild · Bitter	Leaves used in teas, flowers
Passiflora	Passionflower	Leaves · Shoots · Flowers · Fruits	LEAVES Mild spinach FLOWERS Sweet FRUIT Sour · Sweet	Stir fry the leaves, use the flowers in herbal teas and as a garnish
Pelargonium	Scented Geranium	Leaves · Flowers	LEAVES Strong perfumed FLOWERS Mild · Taste according to variety	Use the leaves and flowers to flavour sugar, syrups, liqueurs, cream puddings and cakes
Phlox paniculata	Perennial phlox	Flowers	Sweet · Violet	Infuse into apple jellies (see page 137) Serve in salads, and on desserts as an edible flower
Robinia pseudoacacia	Robinia / False Acacia tree	Flowers	Sweet · Honey · Pea	Use as Wisteria
Tulipa	Tulip	Petals	Pea	Use the petals as a canapé base, blend with salts to make a tulip seasoning, ferment in pickles like Camellia and turnip
Viola	Pansy violas & violets	Flowers	Sweet violets have a classic parma violet flavour. Other violas are mildly sweet	Use the flowers on cakes and desserts as a garnish; fresh or sugared. Use the leaves and flowers in salads
Viola odorata	Sweet violet	Flowers · Leaves	FLOWERS Parma · Violet LEAVES Mild · Nutty	Use the flowers in liqueurs (crème de violette), vinegar and chocolate on cakes as a garnish. Use the leaves and flowers in salads

Published in 2024
by Hardie Grant Books,
an imprint of Hardie Grant Publishing

Hardie Grant Books (London)
5th & 6th Floors
52–54 Southwark Street
London SE1 1UN

Hardie Grant Books (Melbourne)
Building 1, 658 Church Street
Richmond, Victoria 3121
hardiegrantbooks.com

British Library Cataloguing-in-Publication Data. A catalogue record for this book is available from the British Library.

Buds & Blossoms
ISBN: 9781784886592

10 9 8 7 6 5 4 3 2 1

PUBLISHING DIRECTOR
Kajal Mistry

SENIOR EDITOR
Chelsea Edwards

ART DIRECTION
Evi-O.Studio | Susan Le

DESIGN ASSISTANT
Evi-O.Studio | Matt Crawford

ILLUSTRATIONS
Evi-O.Studio | Siena Zadro

COVER DESIGN
Stuart Hardie

PHOTOGRAPHER
Kim Lightbody

PHOTOGRAPHER'S ASSISTANT
Marie Campain

PROP STYLIST
Rachel Vere

FOOD STYLIST
Esther Clark

FOOD STYLIST'S ASSISTANT
Clare Cole

COPYEDITOR
Emily Preece-Morrison

PROOFREADER
Vicky Orchard

INDEXER
Helen Snaith

PRODUCTION CONTROLLER
Martina Georgieva

Colour reproduction by p2d
Printed and bound in China by
Leo Paper Products Ltd.

FSC www.fsc.org
MIX
Paper | Supporting responsible forestry
FSC™ C020056